T0330163

Public Sector Enterprise Resource Planning

Public Sector Enterprise Resource Planning

Issues in Change Management

Edited by

Rainer A. Sommer

Enterprise Engineering Laboratory
George Mason University, USA

Edward Elgar
Cheltenham, UK • Northampton, MA, USA

Published by
Edward Elgar Publishing Limited
Glensanda House
Montpellier Parade
Cheltenham
Glos GL50 1UA
UK

Edward Elgar Publishing, Inc.
William Pratt House
9 Dewey Court
Northampton
Massachusetts 01060
USA

A catalogue record for this book
is available from the British Library

Library of Congress Cataloguing in Publication Data

Public sector enterprise resource planning : issues in change management/
edited by Rainer Sommer.
    p. cm.
  Includes bibliographical references and index.
1. Administrative agencies–United States–Management. 2. Management
information systems–United States. 3. Administrative
agencies–Technological innovations–Management. 4. Government
productivity–United States. 5. Business Planning. I. Sommer, Rainer,
1956-
  JK468.A8P835 2006
  352.3'4–dc22

ISBN-13: 978 1 84542 006 2
ISBN-10: 1 84542 006 3

Printed and bound in Great Britain by MPG Books Ltd, Bodmin, Cornwall

Contents

PART III RESEARCH VIEW

List of Contributors

Daniel L. Cuda is a Research Staff member at the Institute for Defense Analyses in Alexandria, Virginia. His areas of interest are the confluence of public sector organizational theory, performance budgeting, and information. He previously graduated from Georgetown University and the US Air Force Academy, and is a veteran of the 1990 Gulf War. His areas of expertise are national security policy and its resource allocation processes.

Dr. Douglas W. Frye is a consultant with several years of experience in public policy issue analysis, focusing on space and information technologies. Dr. Frye currently supports the Army Material Command (AMC) Single Army Logistics Enterprise effort. Dr. Frye received his Ph.D. in Public Policy-Organizational Informatics from George Mason University in 2004.

Mary A. Leary is a Doctoral Researcher specializing in projects that include best practices in enterprise solutions implementation, transportation strategic planning, and public/private partnerships with a focus on various public health projects. Ms. Leary is also a policy analyst in the Department of Health and Human Services and an advocate for long-term care reform. Her academic career includes earning a Bachelor of Science Degree from James Madison University and a Master of Administrative Science degree from Johns Hopkins University.

Micheline Lopez-Estrada is currently a Managing Consultant specializing in strategic planning and acquisition and technical oversight of enterprise business architecture implementations in support of Federal Agencies. Ms. Lopez-Estrada has 13 years experience of government service with the Department of the Navy and was the Business Process Manager for the Enterprise Solutions Program Office on Project SIGMA at Naval Aviation from July 2000 to January 2003. Ms. Lopez-Estrada holds a Bachelor of Science degree in Computer Science from the Interamerican University of Puerto Rico and an additional 5-year Bachelor of Science degree in Computer Engineering from the University of Puerto Rico-Mayaguez Campus. She also holds two graduate degrees; one in Business Administration from the Florida Institute of Technology and the other is a Master of Science in Technical Management from Johns Hopkins University.

Grayson Morgan is a Department of Defense engineer in the field of Information Assurance, and has spent the last 15 years in government/military service developing communication systems operational requirements. Although employed as a data flow specialist with the intelligence community and cryptologist in the Naval Reserves, his focus continues to show how technology impacts military decision processes. Gray holds a Bachelor of Science degree in systems engineering from the Naval Academy, a Master of Public Administration from Georgia College and State University, a Master of Arts in Government from Johns Hopkins University, and certification as a Federal Chief Information Officer.

David Bailey is a Senior Enterprise Architect working for the US Army in support of several SAP process alignment functions and SAP Solution Manager Integration. In that capacity he manages a small team of process architects who are responsible for developing process-based scenarios that align with the SAP Solution Manager process repository. Mr. Bailey has completed SAP certified training courses and has implemented and managed several SAP 4.6c system environments. Mr. Bailey holds a Bachelor of Individualized Study degree (Enterprise Engineering) from George Mason University.

Dr. Matthias Kirchmer is CEO of IDS Scheer North America, the leading provider of business process excellence solutions. Dr. Kirchmer, a renowned expert in business process management, is a member of the Extended Executive Board of IDS Scheer AG, and also heads up the Japanese operations of IDS Scheer. Dr. Kirchmer has been instrumental in designing and implementing business processes, as well as directing numerous business process improvement initiatives, including multiple process-orientated software implementations. He joined IDS Scheer in 1990 as a consultant. Under the guidance of Dr. August-Wilhelm Scheer, founder and Chairman of IDS Scheer, Dr. Kirchmer developed a deep understanding of business processes and how they are related to a broad range of industries. Dr. Kirchmer has successfully executed multiple business process management projects, including multiple SAP software implementations. Since 1993, he had been responsible for standard software implementation consulting activities, with a focus on SAP. He is an affiliated faculty member of the Center for Organizational Dynamics of the University of Pennsylvania.

Lt. Col. Robert Russell has been directly involved in a number of organizational design activities and implementations in the Canadian Forces. Significant amongst these, were those initiatives he was responsible for as the Senior Resource Manager for Land Forces in the Atlantic Area. During this time, he also completed his Executive Master of Business Administration adding to his experiences with change management issues in the public sector. Lt.Col. Russell is currently employed on liaison staff at US Army Material Command Headquarters.

Dr. Lisa K. Westerback is the Director of the Office of Information Technology Policy and Planning in the Office of the Chief Information Officer, US Department of Commerce. She is responsible for developing and promulgating Department-wide information technology policy and for directing the information technology planning and investment review, e-government, and enterprise information technology architecture programs for the Department of Commerce. She holds an Arts Bachelor in Economics from Smith College, a Master of Arts in International Affairs and a Master of Philosophy in Economics, both from the George Washington University, and a Doctorate in Public Administration from the University of Southern California.

Dr. Thomas Gulledge is Professor of Public Policy and Engineering at George Mason University and Director of the Policy Analysis Center. Dr. Gulledge is the Director of the Ph.D. concentration in Organizational Informatics within the School of Public Policy, and a cofounder of the Master of Science program in Enterprise Engineering. He is the Director of the corporate sponsored International Electronic Commerce project, with partners Oracle Corporation, Great Plains Software, IDS-Scheer, SAP, and Promatis. He is also the Program Manager for a series of ongoing funded initiatives relating to supply chain integration, and international electronic commerce in Europe and Asia.

Dr. Rainer A. Sommer is Associate Professor of Public Policy and Enterprise Engineering as well as the Assistant Director of the Policy Analysis Center of the George Mason University School of Public Policy. He currently serves as the director of the George Mason University Master of Science in Enterprise Engineering Program. While employed at George Mason University he has held several research and teaching positions in the fields of Business-to-Business (B2B) electronic commerce and supply chain integration, international telecommunication, Enterprise Resource Planning (ERP) system implementation and design, and most recently ERP-based business process engineering methods.

Cheryl A. Darlington is an Enterprise Architect working for the US Army Material Command in support of ERP implementation planning and business process modeling. She has extensive experience in the design and implementation of cross-functional business process architectures and has recently completed her Master of Science in Enterprise Engineering from George Mason University.

Dr. Carsten Svensson specializes in the analysis and design of product life-cycle management systems. He has extensive experience in cross-functional process integration and ERP-based implementation methodologies. Dr. Svensson is currently employed as a Senior Enterprise Architect in support of the Army Material Command SAP implementation effort. Dr. Svensson received his Ph.D. in Manufacturing Engineering from the Technical University of Denmark.

Georg Simon is Director of Consulting at IDS Scheer in Berwyn, Pennsylvania. Mr. Simon has consulted internationally on the efficacy of cross-functional business process design and integrated ERP system implementation. Mr. Simon has extensive experience in the managerial and technical implementation aspects of the SAP business solution and has consulted on these issues with many multi-national firms. Mr. Simon also served as the lead engineer for IDS-Prof. Scheer AG in the development of the ARIS toolset – one of the world's leading integrated business process engineering software packages. Mr. Simon holds a Dipl.Ing. in Electrical Engineering from the Fachhochschule fuer Technik und Wirtschaft in Germany.

Preface

The Federal enterprise is large and complex. Hence, the implementation of Enterprise Resource Planning (ERP) systems at the Federal level has not enjoyed the same success rate as in the private sector. In this book we assert that the Federal government will eventually change the way it manages non-unique business processes. The declining resource base will not support the existing infrastructure, but even if resources were plentiful, there would still be strong incentive to change. New IT-enabled process management methodologies have been implemented worldwide, and organizations are achieving enhanced efficiency and effectiveness through the use of these new management approaches. Since 2000, these new approaches have been spreading to the public sector, and the US Department of Defense is an early implementer and a leader for other public organizations.

Appropriate models and systems have been implemented in the private sector, and throughout this book we attempt to identify specific challenges that public sector managers must overcome and to learn from private sector experiences. Private sector implementations have led to competitive advantage, better management control, and cost reductions. While public sector incentives and performance measures are different from the private sector, better management control and cost reductions are certainly public sector objectives.

The authors present several expertly researched Federal, commercial, and academic views on how public sector organizations are integrating their business processes, and they make every effort to draw comparisons to the private sector experience. The intent is to describe several public sector management models that are consistent with private sector models, and to demonstrate how the models should be implemented. The discussion covers all aspects of the new private sector management paradigm, ranging from strategic planning, change management, process change, and information system implementation. The authors provide details on the implementation steps, and make suggestions on how public sector program managers and contractor teams should plan to change management and ERP initiatives.

Most of the articles draw heavily on personal experiences garnered while working on large-scale public sector ERP and change management initiatives. However, some critical issues can only be discussed within the context of performance-oriented private sector initiatives, where competitive advantage is the driving factor in influencing such radical organizational changes.

However, it is clear that government is managed differently than the private sector. The performance measures and incentives are distinctly different. There are no public sector performance measurement equivalents for 'profitability' and 'return-on-investment', and public managers have a special obligation to wisely spend tax dollars. However, there are many public sector processes that are equivalent to private sector business processes. Although considered mundane, they represent the most basic processes that are essential for sustaining an enterprise.

Although surprising to some public sector vested interests, there is nothing special about the management of public organizations that preclude them from implementing modern private sector management practices and integrated ERP systems. Although performance measures and incentives may be different, public sector business processes are essentially the same as their commercial counterparts. The need for accurate and timely management information is just as urgent in the public sector as in the private sector. Hence, there is no reason the information systems that support common business processes should not be the same across public and private sector enterprises.

If the public sector does not learn from the private sector, there is a good chance that the cost efficiency and accounting accuracy demanded by congress will not be forthcoming and thus it will be increasingly difficult to effectively sustain high-value government organizations and processes.

R.A. Sommer
George Mason University
June 2006

PART I

PUBLIC SECTOR VIEW

1. Battlespace ERP Systems: Changing the Way Military Decision Makers Think in a Net-Centric Information Environment

Grayson Morgan

INTRODUCTION

Armed conflict is the ultimate test of any enterprise resource planning (ERP) system where the availability of information to military personnel regarding vital Department of Defense (DoD) resources can mean the difference between a battle won and a battle lost. This revolution in communications technology is changing the fundamental process of military command and control and has initiated a transformation in combat operations toward the creation of a net-centric information environment (NCIE). Designed to 'improve vertical and horizontal intelligence distribution'[1] by integrating warfighters with the Pentagon's globally distributed information enterprise (Figure 1.1), the NCIE goal of creating decision superiority through real time ERP interaction does so by overlooking critical aspects of the tactical decision making process. This basic failure to see beyond technical application will take us down an uncharted path with the deadliest of consequences.

Never before have battlespace decision makers had access to such staggering amounts of tactical, operational, and strategic information, proportions that continue to increase faster than the ability of either man or machine to utilize effectively. While commanders struggle to fuse the seemingly endless streams of digital data from current DoD ERP databases within the dynamics of armed combat, they are quickly discovering how already narrow windows for decisive action continue to shrink in the face of enhanced situational awareness. Military planners must take advantage of rapidly evolving technology to lift the 'fog of greater or lesser uncertainty'[3] that hangs over every combat operation. However, the current process of merely networking current ERP systems with questionable database integrity will likely induce unevaluated risks and ultimately affect judgment quality.

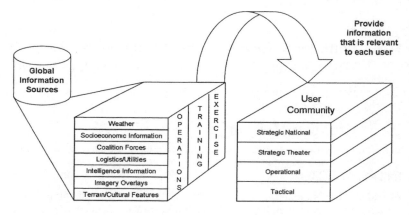

Figure 1.1: Global Command and Control Information Integration[2]

Establishing the 'As Is'

The nature of the way information can be gathered and analyzed to yield knowledge superiority has been transformed by technology.[4]

Air Chief Marshal Sir Brian Burridge

ENTERPRISE RESOURCE PLANNING

A great number of people familiar with commercial ERP systems such as SAP, PeopleSoft, and Oracle may wonder where the connection exists between business-oriented software and the military commander in the field. While military organizations have used ERP systems for years to enhance 'administrative' functions (i.e. non-combat, business-like activities such as control of resources, personnel management, logistics, and training), recent advances in network and communication technology have made such information processes available to 'operational' forces in every type of battlespace currently being utilized. Because ERP applications help integrate 'information across functions, and provide a set of tools for planning and monitoring the various functions and processes',[5] their use in focusing organizational activities to enhance military tactics can produce extraordinary results. As such, the ERP process is a rapidly expanding capability becoming available to an increasing number of combat ready units in today's high information decision environments.

SAP promotes its commercially available software solutions as giving 'real-time visibility across your entire enterprise, so you can streamline your supply chain, bring products to market faster, get more out of procurement, and eliminate duplication of effort'.[6] Within military circles, operational ERP tools are known collectively as part of the Global Command and Control System (GCCS) family of systems incorporating Unix and Windows based applications designed to manage combat-related data and intelligence information.

Like its commercial counterparts, GCCS (pronounced 'geeks') is designed to provide warfare commanders with real-time visibility across a specific military service's worldwide operational enterprise, streamline the information supply chain, bring joint combat arms to the battlespace faster, get more 'bang for the buck', and eliminate redundancies between the armed services. This is the same process utilized by industry, but with a slightly different application.

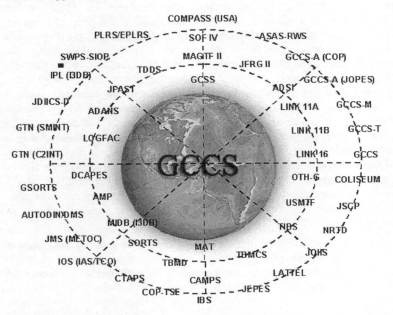

Figure 1.2: Global Command and Control Interfaces [7]

Unfortunately, the Army, Navy, Air Force, and Joint Forces Command have developed their own systems with varying degrees of interoperability due to unique hardware and software configurations. For example, the

Navy's version is known as GCCS-Maritime and has four different variants for ashore, afloat, tactical, and joint commands with nearly 400 units/platforms linked together. In order to provide the required level of situational awareness needed by military commanders, GCCS-Maritime fuses data from no fewer than 80 different combat systems such as weapons, precision targeting tools, mission planning tools, cryptology assets, and sensor platforms. In turn, the critical information provided by these systems is linked through a common GCCS-Maritime interface to the overall command and control network where it can be utilized in conjunction with other DoD information systems (Figure 1.2).

Information Integrity

While database interoperability between the different service GCCSs is an important factor in solidifying the Pentagon's overall network functionality, the integrity of information within these databases is pivotal to the establishment of a trusted NCIE. The fundamental inability of ERP system administrators to maintain this trust lies at the heart of the Pentagon's dilemma regarding NCIE implementation. While understanding the multifaceted concept of 'data integrity' may be a difficult, mathematically challenging experience, some level of comprehension by DoD policy makers is necessary if any type of meaningful solution is to be implemented.

Dr. Amihai Motro, an expert on information systems at George Mason University, presents a straightforward explanation of database integrity covering both the concept of integrity and the mathematics behind it in a paper entitled 'Integrity = Validity + Completeness'. According to Dr. Motro's research, any data sets provided by an ERP 'have integrity if they contain the whole truth (completeness) and nothing but the truth (validity)'.[8] Since real world environments are subject to change and the database must change accordingly, the integrity of most databases is violated routinely in one of two ways (Figure 1.3):

- A known truth in the real world is not reflected by the database (completeness);
- A known truth within the database is not reflective of the real world (validity).

A practical element of maintaining database integrity is the understanding that administrators must continually monitor both the real world and the system in order to compare the two for differences and authorize changes. As much as standard convention would like us to believe the integrity of an ERP database is more or less assured if proper security measures are taken, Dr.

Motro believes human supervision is still required for two compelling reasons:

- Database systems cannot determine whether all data entered is true or false; if they could, then violation detection would be completely automatic and the update rejected.
- Database systems cannot sense every change in the real world; if they could, then violations could be detected automatically and the database would update itself accordingly.[9]

Areas of Violation

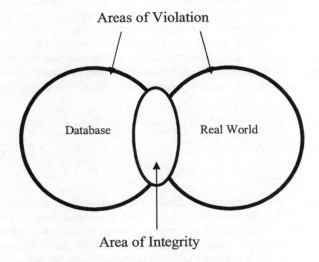

Area of Integrity

Figure 1.3: Sources of Validity and Completeness

The reality of this problem is an everyday issue for military ERP system administrators. According to Captain Robert Craig, assistant chief of staff with Naval Security Group Reserve for Communications and Information systems, 'Questions on data [integrity] must go back to the source as discrepancies are currently caught via visual inspection'.[10] While this type of solution is extremely inefficient in terms of both time and resources, commands throughout the Department of Defense are routinely forced to manually 'scrub' the database systems under their control. Try as they might to prevent data corruption, these personnel are in a constant struggle to purge inaccurate data and most have made the review process an integral part of their ERP's standard operating procedure.

Security is not Integrity

In the public sector, where acquisition program parameters are defined by lawyers and verified by legal counsel, knowing the meaning of a word or concept and attempting to act upon that definition is usually a difficult undertaking at best. The definition of information assurance (IA) developed by the National Security Agency (NSA) to 'protect and defend' essential elements of both information and information systems is designed to ensure availability, integrity, authentication, confidentiality, and non-repudiation (i.e., accountability).[11] The goal of the IA process is to enhance user trust, but the level of that trust is limited and not always well understood.

As the undisputed government authority on information security, it is no wonder NSA's definition of information assurance is the only one used by the Pentagon as a framework to support its ERP integrity policy. Focusing attention solely on the 'integrity' aspect of IA and the definition for it provided by the Committee on National Security Systems, the following components of today's database integrity are simple and straightforward:

- Correctness and reliability of the operating system;
- Completeness of the hardware and software implementing the protection mechanisms;
- Consistency of the data structures and occurrence of the stored data;
- Protection against unauthorized modification or destruction of information.[12]

Those in the database management field will quickly realize something amiss about this particular definition. After a momentary review, it becomes obvious that every aspect of the operating systems, hardware, software, data structures, and proper usage are covered, but no mention is made regarding the data itself. From this definition, the Pentagon's goal for maintaining ERP data integrity has been and will continue to be the creation of reliable, impregnable computer networks capable of receiving, storing, manipulating, and transmitting data to and from authorized users regardless of the information's accuracy. In effect, the DoD policy has facilitated the creation of a highly secure GIGO (Garbage In, Garbage Out) apparatus.[13]

It is an established axiom of the computer age that if invalid data is entered into a system for action, the resulting output will be equally invalid along with any decision tainted by its use. While there is no evidence to suggest electronic sensors or personnel are filling the military's ERP databases with massive amounts of flawed data, it does illustrate how the current IA definition assumes either perfect data or dismisses the impact of its existence. Not only do such assumptions contradict the military operating environment, they simultaneously exclude any requirement to prevent erroneous data from being inadvertently injected into critical information systems.

Force in Transition

Network-centric warfare is not about technology per se, it is an emerging theory of war. It is not about the network, rather it is about how wars are fought. During the industrial age, power came from mass. Now power tends to come from information, access and speed.[14]

Vice Admiral Arthur K. Cebrowski

Global War On Terrorism

Successful change management involving IA and risk analysis of the NCIE concept can only be achieved if the context for change is part of the answer. With the transformation of our military's command and control capabilities mandated by top-level leadership, the first question we need to ask ourselves is: 'Why'? Within the Department of Defense, the need to evolve beyond current organizational methods given recent lessons learned from the activities of Operation Enduring Freedom and Operation Iraqi Freedom has proven an essential ingredient for change. Since the end of the first Gulf War, military planners have studied the effects of increased battlefield connectivity on such key enterprise services as command and control, training, logistics, and joint combat (i.e. the use of combined Army/Navy/Air Force/Marine Corps services or multi-national assets). Comparing events from a decade ago with those of the last two years indicates a profound correlation between integration and joint effectiveness.

While reviewing past actions to acquire insight for future process improvement is not a new concept to military strategists, the Pentagon's Joint Center for Operations Analysis–Lessons Learned chose to evaluate the war on terrorism differently in response to dramatic changes between the battlespace of past engagements and the battlespace of today. Speed is the new watchword for current military doctrine and information pulled from a range of ERP systems is the fuel powering our forces in the new joint warfare environment. According to the Center's director, Army Brigadier General Robert Cone, the difference between past evaluations and ongoing analysis resides not in the technology, but in the methodology.[15]

The history of warfare tells us military officials have routinely looked for clues at improving their doctrine and policy through systematic reviews of events after the fact. General Cone believed this type of 'post-mortem' evaluation, conducted only once the fighting had ceased, lacked the essential context required to fully understand the needs of the warfighter. In order to capture the true essence of those needs and the vital role of information to the decision maker, US Joint Forces Command (USJFCOM) took the unprecedented step of imbedding observers at command and control centers across the entire theater of conflict prior to the start of military operations: Qatar, Saudi Arabia, Bahrain, Afghanistan, and among supporting government agencies in Washington D.C.

Despite the reluctance of any organization to increase self-scrutiny for the sake of implementing change management, this difficulty was eased by the assignment becoming more than an exercise in "look, but don't touch" as observers took an active role in advising field commanders and their staffs. The Pentagon was changing the way it evaluated change and the mission from General Cone was clear: 'If you can fix something, you ought to intervene'.[16] For the first time in US history, war was to be studied as a dynamic assessment by capturing not only how decisions are made and the information upon which they are based, but also the collaborative process behind this dynamic interaction.

In the three month period of March to May 2003, thousands of hours of observation, over 600 interviews with personnel engaged in operations, and more than 80 gigabytes of situational data have provided the analysts at Joint Forces Command with a truly remarkable snapshot of battlespace information usage and effectiveness. The array of information made available to the decision maker and the creation of a virtual collaborative environment designed to enhance the application of joint forces became evident when compared with past conflicts (Figure 1.4).

While bandwidth availability in the NCIE demonstrated an ability to increase combat capabilities (combined arms, precision weapons, etc.), the quality of the decisions and the operational processes used to achieve the desired goals repeatedly showed signs of weakness. According to Admiral Edmund Giambastiani, commander of US Joint Forces Command, although enhanced battlespace capabilities demonstrated considerable effectiveness, they also demonstrated severe limitations and a need for 'substantial improvements'.[18] Due to changes in the decision making process and the increase in time limitations, these weaknesses become even more profound when the NCIE is utilized away from higher level operational commanders and moved closer to the more dynamic tactical battlespace.

A New Integrity

As the Pentagon's back office ERP processes move closer to the front line of military operations, it should be no surprise to see the value of information change between tactical, operational, and strategic environments. Acknowledgment of this continuous shift was recognized in a more holistic view of information assurance proposed by Dr. Yacov Haimes, an expert in critical infrastructure protection at the University of Virginia. From his perspective, information assurance and its components are resource capable of increasing or decreasing as survivability measures dictate. As such, data integrity must be viewed as an asset utilizing several disciplines to include:

- Risk assessment and management;
- Human and organizational behavior;
- Business management.[19]

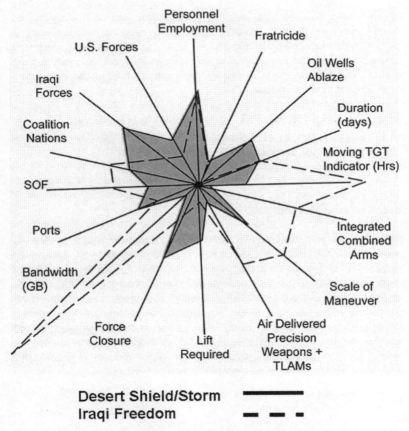

Figure 1.4: Comparisons of Warfare[17]

According to Dr. Haimes' broadened definition of IA, 'accuracy indicating a level of information integrity'[20] can be represented as a state-of-the-system attribute similar to a database's storage capacity or transfer rate. While the presence of inaccurate data is a common occurrence in administrative ERP systems, any level of false data in an operational system supporting real-time tactical engagements would be intolerable. The creation of metadata (i.e. data about data) integrity attribute scales could provide networked systems with a universal standard easily interpreted by those decision makers with increased data accuracy requirements.

Since future database systems are unlikely to achieve one hundred percent accuracy anytime soon, the ability of the data user to gage the relative integrity of the information presented could be a decisive factor in the decision making process. However difficult it may be, implementing a government wide definition change for integrity to include a weighting schema would go far towards enhancing user trust of available information systems and help to shore up one of the weakest areas of the Pentagon's existing ERP implementation policy.

THE FUTURE OF BATTLESPACE MANAGEMENT

> You can bring all the new technologies you want, but if you cannot change how you think, you will not achieve transformation.[21]

Air Force Major General Marc Rogers

Universal Interoperability

Central to the transformation of US military capabilities allowing them to operate in a NCIE is the creation of a new, more integrated ERP network to replace the stove-piped GCCS systems currently fielded throughout the Department of Defense. This new format, outlined within the Joint Battle Management Command and Control (JBMC2) Roadmap, is envisioned to be the Pentagon's policy and technology integration vehicle for 'prioritizing, aligning, and synchronizing' twenty two planned JBMC2 architectural and acquisition efforts. The development of JBMC2 is a direct result of the lessons learned during the Global War on Terrorism and is specifically designed to reduce joint interoperability problems through increases in:

- Real-time and commonly shared situational awareness;
- Decision superiority;
- The ability to conduct distributed operations.

While current GCCS capabilities originated as independently fielded service programs sharing limited or no interfaces, the new JBMC2 system will consist of 'joint mission capability packages and Service-unique applications based on Global Information Grid (GIG) enterprise services designed to enable shared access to Service/Agency/joint-provided data sources'.[22] Service-unique processes will be limited to only service-unique applications and will still be required to incorporate as many of the JBMC2 standards as possible. In layman's terms, DoD procurement across the board is now required to follow the new network protocol (i.e., GIG) standards for the creation of DoD wide database access.

As far as scope is concerned, JBMC2 will touch every aspect of the Pentagon's current and planned information network. The new 'joint philosophy' of information sharing will depend predominantly on a host of common core 'joint applications', defined by 'joint standards' that make use of a common GIG compliant 'joint computing and communications infrastructure'.[23] Using a descriptive measure any ERP implementation manager will understand, the total cost of JBMC2 throughout the Department of Defense between fiscal years 2004 and 2009 has been estimated at more than US $47 Billion and continues to grow.[24]

According to General Rogers, the overall goal of creating JBMC2 is to achieve a 'complete and seamless integration of DoD service, interagency, and multinational capabilities'.[25] The integrated set of JBMC2 capabilities, specifically the net-centric communications and information services derived from the GIG, will form the foundation of the JBMC2 program and enable forces to access vast information resources from one of the GIG's ten net-centric core enterprise services. Number eight on the list of services is Information Assurance and Security.

False Assurance
In a seamless joint force network infrastructure, 'even the best-designed architectures, software, and systems may be flawed in subtle ways and subject to unforeseen interoperability problems'.[26] According to the Roadmap, the transition to network-based JBMC2 services at the tactical level can only be implemented if the future capabilities provided to the warfighter include guarantees of data integrity, consistency, and assurance. The problem that exists for the JBMC2, although not so 'unforeseen' to front line combatants, lies within the truncated decision making process of the tactical environment.

While the JBMC2 system will provide a host of services on demand for tactical operations, it will come at the cost of using data of questionable validity. As mentioned earlier, the GIG is designed to provide the standardized software and technical interfaces upon which JBMC interoperability is achieved; however, tactical net-centric data integrity will not be sufficient given the inappropriate application of information assurance strategies. The strategies discussed throughout the Roadmap were designed for the security of the network itself.

The JBMC2 Data Strategy mentioned in the Roadmap, a derivative of the DoD Net-Centric Data Strategy, was conceived to fill this obvious discrepancy by providing the managerial and technical infrastructure needed to achieve data integrity. Unfortunately, the strategy's goal of maintaining trusted data using the exceptionally vague solutions of 'pedigrees and security metadata and authoritative sources'[27] is simply not enough. Security metadata is already an IA practice used to increase data authenticity (data sent being the same as that received), not integrity; and the use of 'pedigrees' and 'authoritative sources' makes the improper assumption that ERP data, by the very nature of the GIG network from which it operates, is valid and complete.

CONCLUSIONS

The full impact of a technological solution to an organizational problem is often not fully understood; its impact on the people and culture as well as work processes needs to be investigated fully before and during design and implementation.[28]

Dr. Athanasia Pouloudi

ERP implementation is about change management and if the Department of Defense can change how information is integrated with operational requirements, it can change the metrics of its command and control systems with regard to data integrity. First, without a proper working definition for data integrity within the scope of IA, no amount of program support or technical development will satisfy end user requirements. This is particularly true for the warfighter linked to an ERP database via the GIG. Change is essential for creating a proper frame of reference as the difference between system integrity and data integrity has blurred to the point that many believe they are one in the same. Continued use of the existing NSA definition designed to assure information systems will increase the problematic assumption that data within a secure computer network is correct simply because it is protected. It cannot be stressed enough how each represents an entirely unique aspect of the NCIE.

Second, the problem of data integrity must be acknowledged and processes to prevent, detect, and correct operational ERP database corruption established as part of the net-centric transformation effort. While many would say the existing level of data integrity maintained by the Pentagon seems to work well enough, those individuals would likely decline the responsibility of making life and death decisions if they knew the system is not one hundred percent accurate. Unfortunately, this happens to be the case as with all information systems.

Finally, attempting to provide real-time military ERP systems such as GCCS and JBMC2 with unquestionable data integrity in today's dynamic real world environment would be impossible to achieve and a waste of limited resources. A balanced solution focused on high standards and visual indications of the data's integrity level would allow decision makers to evaluate net-centric information uniformly either as an individual or within a collaborative group. While many automated processes provide some type of database validation to prevent database errors, these measures are not perfect and open the doorway to erroneous decision making unless an integrity weighting of some type is provided to the user.

The purpose of these changes in the existing ERP implementation process is to allow the warfighter to make the best possible judgment using the information available. Although decisions are routinely made with reduced data integrity, the false security and unknown risks associated with current policies may ultimately prove the undoing of ERP systems on the front lines.

NOTES

1. Donald Rumsfeld, Legislative Priorities for Fiscal Year 2005. Memorandum, 24 Sept., 2003.
2. Joint Forces Command Collaborative Information Environment Concept Primer, Oct., 2003, pg 2.
3. Carl von Clausewitz, On War, Michael E. Howard and Peter Paret, eds., Princeton, NJ: Princeton University Press, 1976, p. 101.
4. The Windsor Leadership Trust Annual Lecture at Savoy Place, London, 19 November 2003.
5. www.managementsupport.com
6. www.sap.com/solutions
7. http://jitc.fhu.disa.mil/gccsiop/index.html
8. Motro, Amihai, 'Integrity = Validity + Completeness', ACM Transactions on Database Systems, Vol. 14, No. 4, December 1989, p. 480.
9. Motro, Amihai, 'Integrity = Validity + Completeness', ACM Transactions on Database Systems, Vol. 14, No. 4, December 1989, p. 487.
10. Briefing at prospective commanding officer/executive officer course on 18 July 2004.
11. National Information Assurance (IA) Glossary, CNSS Instruction No. 4009, revised May 2003, p. 32.
12. National Information Assurance (IA) Glossary, CNSS Instruction No. 4009, revised May 2003, p. 34.
13. www.webopedia.com
14. Presentation to USArmy War College, 29 October 2003.
15. Briefing on Joint Lessons Learned from Operation Iraqi Freedom by the Director, Joint Center for Lessons Learned, US Joint Forces Command, 2 October 2003.
16. Briefing on Joint Lessons Learned from Operation Iraqi Freedom by the Director, Joint Center for Lessons Learned, US Joint Forces Command, 2 October 2003.
17. Briefing on Joint Lessons Learned from Army Fellows Conference, 31 July 2003.
18. Briefing on Joint Lessons Learned to the US House Armed Services Committee, 2 October 2003.
19. Haimes, Y., Risk Modeling, Assessment, and Management, John Wiley & Sons, New York, NY, 1998.
20. Longstaff, T. and Haimes, Y., Education and Knowledge Management: A Requisite For Information Assurance, Information Survivability Workshop, 30 August 2000, p. 1.
21. US Joint Forces Director for Requirements and Integration, Joint Warfare: Transformation and New Requirements conference, 22 June 2004.
22. Joint Forces Command Space and Decision Superiority Division Overview Brief, 7 May 2004.
23. Joint Command and Control Order (JC2 ORD), 22 August 2003.

24. Joint Battle Management Command and Control Roadmap – Version 2.0, 27 February 2004, p. 33.
25. US Joint Forces Director for Requirements and Integration, Joint Warfare: Transformation and New Requirements conference, 22 June 2004.
26. Joint Battle Management Command and Control Roadmap – Version 2.0, 27 February 2004, p. xvii.
27. Joint Battle Management Command and Control Roadmap – Version 2.0, 27 February 2004, p. 135.
28. Pouloudi, Athanasia et al., 'Organizational Appropriation of Technology: A Case Study', Cognition, Technology & Work, London: Springer-Verlag, 1999, p. 175.

BIBLIOGRAPHY

Haimes, Y., Risk Modeling, Assessment, and Management, John Wiley & Sons, New York, NY, 1998.

Howard, Michael E. and Peter Paret, eds. Carl von Clausewitz, On War, Princeton, NJ: Princeton University Press, 1976.

Longstaff, T. and Haimes, Y., Education and Knowledge Management: A Requisite For Information Assurance, Information Survivability Workshop, 30 August 2000.

Motro, Amihai, 'Integrity = Validity + Completeness', ACM Transactions on Database Systems, Vol. 14, No. 4, December 1989.

Pouloudi, Athanasia et al., Organizational Appropriation of Technology: A Case Study, Cognition, Technology & Work, London: Springer-Verlag, 1999.

2. Enterprise Resource Planning: Commerce Administrative Management System

Lisa K. Westerback

INTRODUCTION

This chapter explores the deployment of Enterprise Resource Planning (ERP) software, specifically financial management software, at the US Department of Commerce. The Commerce Administrative Management System (CAMS) is the integrated financial management system implemented throughout the Department of Commerce. The CAMS program has enabled the Department to meet reporting expectations; improve programmatic outcomes with enhanced information and management features; protect funds from waste, fraud, and abuse; and comply with legislative and administrative requirements. CAMS has increased the overall quality of financial data within the Department and has improved the speed and ease of use of financial data.

US DEPARTMENT OF COMMERCE

The US Department of Commerce is one of the most diverse Federal departments. Our mission is to promote job creation and improve living standards for all American citizens by creating an infrastructure that encourages economic growth, technological competitiveness, and sustainable development. We are responsible for collecting and disseminating economic and demographic statistics that assist the public and private sector, facilitating the use of technology both at home and in the workplace, protecting intellectual property, and supporting the environmental and economic health of US communities.

More specifically, the department provides the basic economic data necessary to develop sound business decisions, producing many of the commonly used economic statistics issued by the US Government. The Department of Commerce also produces information designed to encourage the use of science and technology in the production of consumer goods and services.

In addition, it plays an important role in the nation's global business development. The Department develops and disseminates foreign market research and international trade opportunities through its offices in the US and in 83 foreign countries. In addition, it also monitors and enforces compliance with US trade laws and agreements, and defends American firms from injurious foreign business practices by administering US antidumping and countervailing duty laws.

The oceanic and atmospheric programs at the Department improve the understanding and rational use of the natural environment to further the nation's safety, welfare, security, and commerce. These responsibilities include predicting the weather, charting the seas, and protecting the oceans and coastal areas.

Domestically, the Department promotes long-term business enterprises that create jobs for minority groups and in underdeveloped areas across the United States. These programs are supported by reports, publications, projections, and business expertise. The Department provides services to citizens and private business as well as to state, local, and tribal governments.

To carry out this mission, the Department has identified three strategic goals and one management integration goal with specific performance goals supporting each of these strategic goals.

- Strategic Goal 1: Provide the information and tools to maximize US competitiveness and enable economic growth for American industries, workers and consumers.
- Strategic Goal 2: Foster science and technological leadership by protecting intellectual-property, enhancing technical standards and advancing measurement science.
- Strategic Goal 3: Observe, protect and manage the Earth's resources to promote environmental stewardship.
- Management Integration Goal: Achieve organizational and management excellence.

The fiscal year 2005 budget for the Department of Commerce is US $5.8 billion dollars, of which the information technology (IT) budget is about US $1.5 billion, a large percentage for a Federal agency. The Department employs approximately 39,000 employees in 14 independent operating units. These units have different functions, are geographically dispersed (both nationally and internationally), have separate funding streams, and have diverse Congressional support. This diversity and decentralization characterize the Department's approach to information technology management. Technology needs are very different across the Department, ranging from supercomputers to desktop personal computers.

Legislation, Guidance, and Administration Initiatives

Federal laws and oversight guidance from the Office of Management and Budget, the General Accountability Office, and other organizations direct and characterize management and administrative practices in Federal agencies. A number of laws direct IT management practices, including the Clinger–Cohen Act of 1996, which establishes Chief Information Officers (CIOs) with a seat at the table, i.e., reporting directly to the agency head and defining information technology as a strategic element in mission management. The Clinger-Cohen Act, formerly know as the Information Technology Management Reform Act, incorporates the Paperwork Reduction Act of 1995, a large legislative agenda that addresses use of technology to reduce paperwork burden on the public. The Government Paperwork Elimination Act (GPEA) of 1998 drives E-Government efforts to move beyond paper forms. The Electronic Government Act of 2002 complements the GPEA in supporting use of technology to promote citizen-centered government and includes provisions to address information technology security and privacy. The Government Performance and Results Act of 1993 is the driving force for performance measurement in the US Federal Government. Guidance interpreting these laws is included in Office of Management and Budget (OMB) Circular A-130, Management of Federal Information Resources, and other directives and guidance.

Decisions on IT investments are made within the context of this legislation. Outlined below is Commerce's approach to capital planning and investment control as well as to enterprise IT architecture development in response to legislative mandates in these areas. These IT processes influence all major IT investments, including investments in enterprise resource planning.

Additionally, a number of laws and processes direct financial operations in the Federal Government. These include the Chief Financial Officers Act of 1990, which is intended to bring more effective general and financial management practices to the Federal Government. The Act establishes a financial management oversight structure in the Office of Management and Budget and designates a Chief Financial Officer (CFO) in each executive department and in each major executive agency in the Federal Government.

The Joint Financial Management Improvement Program (JFMIP) is an undertaking of the US Department of the Treasury, the General Accountability Office, the Office of Management and Budget, and the Office of Personnel Management working in cooperation with each other and other agencies to improve financial management practices in government. The Program was given statutory authorization in the Budget and Accounting Procedures Act of 1950. The Program promotes strategies and guides financial management improvement across government; reviews and coordinates central agencies activities and policy promulgations; and acts as catalyst and clearinghouse for sharing and disseminating information about good financial management practices.

Under the Federal Financial Management Improvement Act of 1996, agencies must implement and maintain financial management systems that comply substantially with Federal financial management systems requirements; Federal accounting standards as set by JFMIP; and the US Government Standard General Ledger at the transaction level. The OMB Circular A-127 prescribes policies and standards for executive departments and agencies to follow in developing, operating, evaluating, and reporting on financial management systems.

Under the President's Management Agenda, OMB has initiated E-Government activities, which affect all Federal agencies to a greater or lesser extent. OMB's E-Government Web site states:

> In his February 2002 budget submission to Congress, President Bush outlined a management agenda for making government more focused on citizens and results, which includes expanding Electronic Government – or E-Government. E-Government uses improved Internet-based technology to make it easy for citizens and businesses to interact with the government, save taxpayer dollars, and streamline citizen-to-government communications.

> The President's E-Government Strategy has identified several high-payoff, government-wide initiatives to integrate agency operations and information technology investments. The goal of these initiatives will be to eliminate redundant systems and significantly improve the government's quality of customer service for citizens and businesses.

> The Official Web Site of the President's E-Government Initiatives:
>   http://www.whitehouse.gov/omb/egov/index2.html

The 24 E-Government initiatives approved by the President's Management Council in October 2001 are organized in portfolios including Government to Citizen, Government to Business, and Government to Government. The Internal Efficiency and Effectiveness portfolio, which addresses ERP systems:

> is to apply industry best practices to government. FY 2002 accomplishments initiated business transformation successes by advancing agency partnering, citizen focus, and reduction of stovepipe system, and E-Payroll, through the efforts of multi-agency teams, is initiating the migration of agencies from the present 22 providers to 2 payroll partnerships, with a projected lifecycle cost

savings of $995 million. Integrated Acquisition Environment has resulted in an agency-shareable single vendor-performance file; a single vendor registration area that makes it easier to do business with the Federal Government, and a community platform for the Intra-Governmental Transfers, a significant governmental accounting challenge.

The Official Web Site of the President's E-Government Initiatives:
http://www.whitehouse.gov/omb/egov/internal.htm

In February 2002, the OMB established a Federal Enterprise Architecture Program Office to define an IT architecture for the Federal Government. Using its Federal Enterprise Architecture, the OMB has identified Lines of Business initiatives to seek further opportunities to reduce the cost of government and improve services to citizens through business performance. One of the five Lines of Business is Financial Management.

Capital Planning and Investment Control

The Department of Commerce's Capital Planning and Investment Control (CPIC) program is based on a foundation of Strategic and Operational Information Technology Plans, supported by system business cases. These business cases address performance measures, alternatives analysis, life cycle costs, business and technology architecture, security and privacy controls, acquisition strategy, electronic government, etc.

Within the Department's CPIC process, a key component is the Information Technology Review Board (CITRB). The CITRB acts as a board of directors that advises the Secretary and Deputy Secretary on critical IT matters. The CITRB ensures that proposed investments contribute to the Secretary's strategic vision and mission requirements, employ sound IT investment methodologies, comply with Departmental systems architectures, employ sound security measures, and provide the highest return on the investment or acceptable project risk. Establishment of the CITRB supports IT management improvement goals of the Clinger-Cohen Act and the Paperwork Reduction Act as well as implementing related regulations and guidance, including the President's Management Agenda.

The CITRB is chaired by the Department's CIO and co-chaired by its CFO. Board members include the Budget Director, Procurement Executive, Human Resources Director, Deputy CIO and CFO, and the CIOs of the major operating units (National Oceanic and Atmospheric Administration, Census Bureau, and National Institute of Standards and Technology), and the CIOs from selected smaller operating units (currently the International Trade

Administration and the Bureau of Economic Analysis). Thus the CITRB consists of senior level functional and technology experts.

The Board assesses information technology investments at three phases: selection (at project proposal), control (during project development), and evaluation (post implementation). The Board makes recommendations regarding these information technology investments to the Secretary and Deputy Secretary of Commerce through the CIO and the Budget Director. At the Department of Commerce, this is a mature, respected process with considerable clout and influence.

The Board uses formal evaluation criteria in its deliberations. These criteria address six areas of analysis: basis for investment, program management, risk management, security and privacy, architecture, and Secretarial or Administration goals such as electronic government. These evaluation criteria incorporate the key principles of the performance measurement, paperwork reduction/elimination, and E-Government legislation to form an analytical foundation that supports the assorted provisions through a single, cohesive methodology. Scoring against the criteria is done on a three-tiered green, yellow, and red scale.

The CAMS has long been a subject of CITRB review. From the CITRB inception in 1997, CAMS has been a focus of CITRB attention. The Board recognized the central importance of the success of the CAMS project for the management of Commerce's finances and as a model of how to organize and deploy Department-wide systems.

Federated Enterprise IT Architecture

The Department of Commerce enterprise consists of the mission operating units and support organizations, including all business areas. The Department of Commerce Enterprise IT Architecture (EITA) defines the business and technology requirements to perform the enterprise mission in an efficient, cost effective, and reliable manner. It provides a basis for collaborative initiatives that will enhance mission performance, as well as reduce the cost of new deployments.

The EITA is a federated architecture. The complete EITA is the union of the operating unit architectures plus the Department-wide architecture. The Department-wide architecture is a generalized one rather than a specific one. The top level establishes basic goals and directions, characterizes common systems and services, and defines fundamental standards universal to all departmental organizations. This approach allows the operating units flexibility in their mission specific requirements, while providing greater efficiency and reduced cost for those functions that can be shared. The diverse nature and mission of each operating unit precludes a 'one size fits all' approach, but where common ground exists, an enterprise-wide approach is taken. In this way, each organization can fulfill its mission tasks, and provide the best service to all stakeholders and customers while supporting the overall goals of the Department. What is defined Department-wide largely comes under the rubric of enterprise resource planning and is driven by Commerce's strategic Management Integration goal.

Commerce Administrative Management System

Central to enterprise resource planning at the Department of Commerce is the CAMS, which was initiated in late 1993. The purpose of this system is to comply with key financial management legislation such as the Joint Financial Management Improvement Program and the Government Performance and Results Act, and to ensure that Departmental and operating unit financial management is fundamentally sound to protect funds and assets against waste, fraud, and abuse and to provide more effective cost management.

CAMS was implemented in phases. In the fiscal year (FY) 1999 the Bureau of the Census became the first Departmental operating unit to adopt CAMS as its system of records. The Office of the Secretary (OS), the Office of the Inspector General (OIG), and the Office of Computer Services (OCS) within OS followed in FY 2001, and in FY 2002 CAMS saw further adoption with the Bureau of Economic Analysis (BEA), the Economic Development Administration (EDA), the Economics and Statistics Administration (ESA), and the Minority Business Development Administration (MBDA). The National Oceanic and Atmospheric Administration (NOAA) and Bureau of Industry and Security (BIS) adopted CAMS as their system of records in FY 2003, and in FY 2004 were followed by the National Institute of Standards and Technology (NIST), the Technology Administration (TA), and the National Telecommunications and Information Administration (NTIA). CAMS is now the financial system of record for the above named operating units within the Department.

The implementation of CAMS has improved financial accountability and enabled the Department to meet reporting expectations, improve programmatic outcomes with enhanced information and management features, and protect funds from waste, fraud, and abuse. CAMS has increased the overall quality of financial data within the Department and increased the speed and ease of use of financial data. The various data controls within CAMS help ensure that only accurate and valid financial data can enter the system. CAMS allows for data to be captured at the point of entry and the electronic routing of these data for review and approval. CAMS allows Department managers to make better decisions and provide more efficient management and oversight of Department work by providing accurate, timely, and flexible reports to support management. Department of Commerce program managers are able to execute queries/reports to get real-time financial management data about their projects.

CAMS allow the Department to comply with the Federal Financial Management Improvement Act (FFMIA) and Circular A-127. In addition, CAMS can automatically enforce funds control and prompt pay procedures. Further, the implementation of CAMS addresses material weaknesses identified by auditors at NOAA, Census, and other operating units that were associated with weaknesses in their financial management systems. Through the use of CAMS, the Department of Commerce has, over the past five fiscal years, been able to exhibit greater efficiency in the production of financial reports and receive an unqualified financial opinion. Pre-CAMS financial systems neither complied with the relevant financial management legislation nor effectively managed Departmental assets.

In 2000, to facilitate report generation, the Department introduced a data warehouse to coincide with each core financial system instantiation to address the high demand for management and analyst access to financial data and to alleviate the burden on the on-line transaction database. This approach allows performance enhancements while providing for the independence of the operating units to determine the frequency of refresh. Normally, the data warehouse is refreshed over night, but in critical time periods it can be refreshed instantaneously in the background during the day. The data warehouse contains all the detail of the core financial system but is organized in data marts for rapid query and reporting.

The CAMS project has a well-defined management structure and the CAMS implementation strategy seeks to ensure maximum user involvement at each stage. The CAMS Support Center has prepared a risk reduction and mitigation plan that exists in the form of an internal review report. Because of its considerable impact throughout the Department, the CITRB continues to monitor the ongoing operation of CAMS.

The CAMS program directly supports the Department's management integration goal to achieve organizational and management excellence and the corresponding performance goal to ensure effective resource stewardship in support of the Department's programs by improving financial management through the upgrade of Department systems to fully comply with the Federal laws and regulations. By strengthening the integrity of financial operations and ensuring the accuracy of financial records, timely and reliable information enables management to make sound decisions and effectively utilize the resources at its disposal.

CAMS Architecture

The long-term goal of Department of Commerce's EITA is to bring all Commerce operating units under one set of applications for all common administrative functions, i.e. all enterprise resource planning. This will help to reduce the overall cost of these tasks, increase usability of data through standardization, and leverage acquisition by purchasing on a Departmental scale. CAMS provides the financial component of this overall ERP structure.

The central piece of the CAMS design is the financial accounting and management system, known as the Core Financial System (CFS). Additional functions (as shown in Figure 2.1) integrate to the CFS. CAMS consists of the CFS interfaced with standard Department-wide administrative systems for small purchases, bankcards, time reporting/labor cost distribution, data warehouse, and corporate database. As necessary, additional interfaces have been added such as a grants interface and standard interfaces for accounts payable and accounts receivable.

CAMS Feeder Systems

The original architecture for CAMS was a single integrated system that provided a full enterprise resource planning tool for financial management to the Department. However, because of the rapid and significant changes in technology and capabilities since the CAMS plan was first put forth, the architecture was redesigned to feature a core financial system, with additional components built or purchased as commercial-off-the-shelf (COTS) products and integrated with the core financial system. For any further functional CAMS modules, the Department plans to use commercial products or existing Federal systems, as well as the E-Government solutions as they are identified and become available.

A specific Enterprise Application Integration (EAI) tool has been identified to interface between CAMS and its feeder systems. This minimizes interface costs while ensuring the integrity of the data. This product utilizes a standardized XML schema along with translation services to move data between the various systems in real time. It employs a messaging component that defines the destination of the data and the transaction to be completed.

The administrative tasks include all those shown in Figure 2.1, as well as any new tasks that may be identified in the future. Each software package must be capable of directly interfacing with other Commerce and external systems in compliance with the Commerce Technical Reference Model.

Though CAMS is one software product, the Department has four separate instantiations, employing somewhat different financial rules to accommodate special needs. The separate instantiations plus cross-servicing agreements are as follows: NOAA (cross-servicing BIS), NIST (cross-servicing NTIA and TA as well as operating units serviced by former Departmental financial system – EDA, OS, ESA, MBDA, OIG, OCS), Census, and EDA Grants. The Department is working toward reducing the number of instantiations of CAMS to three in the near future.

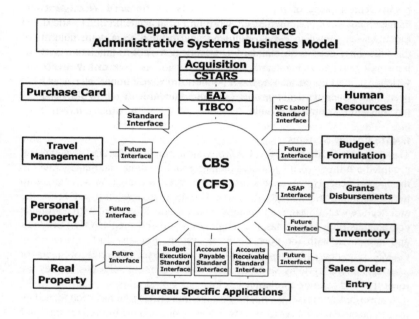

Figure 2.1: CAMS Architecture

Most operating units use CAMS; however, three, the International Trade Administration (ITA), Patent and Trademark Office (PTO), and the National Technical Information Service (NTIS), do not but submit data along with all other units into the Department-wide corporate database that serves as the source for the Department's consolidated financial reports. ITA is serviced by the Interior Department, which employs one of the COTS financial management products. PTO, which is a Performance Based Organization (PBO), also uses this COTS product. PTO's status as a PBO allows it to make independent decisions about administrative management and PTO has chosen a non-CAMS implementation. The NTIS uses a separate system and has been omitted from the CAMS implementation because of its status as a self-supporting organization requiring special financial capabilities, much like PTO. These three organizations feed data to the Commerce corporate database, bringing the Department into compliance with federal financial systems requirements, including that for a single, integrated financial management system.

CAMS Summary Systems

The CAMS corporate database holds all the financial data from the CAMS core financial system as well as the data supplied from the separate ITA, PTO, and NTIS financial systems. It is the repository from which consolidated financial reports are prepared and from which end users can make data queries. Commerce is currently *beta* testing a new COTS product for report generation, which, because it is Web-based, is platform-independent. The system displays a library of the financial management reports that have already been generated and allows access control so that only users who need to see certain information can get to it (Hardy, 2004).

The CAMS Consolidated Reporting System, an executive dashboard, provides a summary view of key financial data, providing an early warning indication for senior managers of the Department's financial status, operating unit by operating unit. The dashboard includes feeds from the financial, human resources, grants, and acquisition systems. The dashboard was not part of the original architecture for CAMS, but came about when the then Deputy Secretary of Commerce bemoaned the lack of financial tools at his government post (Jackson, 2004). The dashboard, also a computer off the shelf (COTS) product, has proven to be a successful management tool. In the near future it will integrate financial and program performance measurement data to meet requirements of the President's Management Agenda.

IT SYSTEM AND CHANGE MANAGEMENT

Impact of Legislation and Oversight

As noted earlier, Federal Government IT system management is controlled or guided by many laws, regulations, and directives. Oversight organizations, both internal and external, make regular reporting demands and conduct reviews, often with specific recommendations that must be completed on a particular time schedule. Financial systems have their own set of guiding legislation and oversight efforts. Thus, decision making regarding IT systems, and particularly, financial systems, is often constrained by legislative or oversight requirements. System development and deployment resources are often derailed to respond to reviews and consequent recommendations. This is an environment that is largely not duplicated in the private sector, allowing private sector organizations more flexibility in IT system deployment including scheduling and resource use.

At the same time, the Department has benefited from the legislation that has mandated CFOs, CIOs, and IT Review Boards. The Department has enjoyed strong CFOs who have exercised leadership and oversight effectively. A recent Federal Times article on ERP notes that 'One problem is that leaders at agencies tend to turn over more frequently than those overseeing companies. So agencies lack long-term leadership than can see through the complete installation of a large enterprise wide software system' (Robb, 2004). Though the Department CFOs have changed over the CAMS development life cycle, all have been committed to the CAMS concept. The CITRB, which includes the CFO and Deputy CFO, has provided a central forum for review of the CAMS effort and ensured steady, consistent direction. The CITRB has exercised strong oversight over CAMS development and deployment, ensuring that the project was restructured when needed and then kept to strict budget allocations and deployment schedules. Further, the CITRB has been a forceful proponent of Department-wide solutions, in general, and a consolidated financial system, in particular.

Impact of Decentralized Environment

As discussed earlier, the Department of Commerce mission is wide and varied, with each operating unit addressing different business lines. The resulting decentralized structure leads to a culture that is often not accepting of enterprise-wide solutions. Operating units, with their separate funding streams, frequently prefer to go their own way and not be constrained to use enterprise-wide systems that may not fit their needs perfectly or may require internal process changes. Use of Department-wide systems has or is perceived to have an additional level of bureaucracy associated with it. However, over time, CAMS has gained acceptance. CAMS' early successes were helpful in supporting acceptance. Formal articulation of the CAMS architecture as part of the Department's enterprise IT architecture also has helped acceptance of CAMS as an enterprise-wide solution. Further, funding shortages have induced senior managers to see the value of cost savings associated with enterprise solutions.

As noted earlier, though CAMS is one software product, the Department has five separate instantiations, employing somewhat different financial rules to accommodate special needs. EDA has agreed to request funds in the fiscal year 2006 to integrate their grants processing with NOAA's CAMS implementation. Though EDA cited a negative return on investment to EDA for this integration, the CITRB members saw the broader Department-wide positive return on investment and recommended that the request proceed.

As explained earlier, ITA has taken a separate path for financial management and is serviced by the Interior Department. This came about because ITA needed to meet certain financial requirements that could not be met through its then-existing financial system, before the CAMS system was ready to accept them. Now that all other CAMS deployments are complete, CAMS is a possible resource for ITA. Concurrently, ITA has identified a need for activity-based accounting and is investigating solutions to meet this need. The CITRB, in its support of enterprise-wide systems, has required that ITA include CAMS in its alternatives analysis for a new solution.

As can be seen from the above two situations, the CITRB has been resolute in requiring the operating units to move toward a single financial standard over time. Without the CFO's leadership and the Board's direction and authority, the Department would still have a wide variety of disparate financial systems and would not have received the management benefits cited earlier.

Internal Process Change Management

The various data controls within the CAMS modules help ensure that only accurate and valid financial data can be entered into the system. A majority of the CAMS screen fields have edits against valid values for a specific field to ensure that erroneous data are not entered into the system for processing. This reduces the time and effort associated with cleaning up invalid entries and processing adjusting entries. CAMS also allows for the data to be captured at the point of entry and the electronic routing of these data for review and approval. Capturing data at end-user entry and electronic routing are far more expedient processes to having someone fill out a form, send it to several individuals for review/approval, and then send the document to a central location where someone else has to key or re-key the data.

The CAMS software, with its stringent edits, forced different management procedures. The burden of accuracy shifted to the original point of entry – errors could not be corrected manually part way through process. This was a painful management lesson, learned first by the Census Bureau. Other operating units benefitted from the Census Bureau's experience and were able to train and inform staff and their managers about the change in operations and the impact on the entry point staff. Specifically, the operating unit program offices have established change management processes and procedures to educate their personnel on why the changes are required, the advantages and benefits of the new system, how the changes will affect each operating unit, and how to reduce/minimize resistance to the new system. In addition, each operating unit has conducted formally structured 'as is' and 'to be' business process analyses, which facilitate change management. The operating units have also conducted conference room pilots with users to ensure the system can conduct business in an acceptable manner.

Along with the change management processes, the program offices have developed comprehensive training programs for both headquarters and regional office staff to facilitate the implementation of new CAMS modules. Activities include having end users participate in testing the software before release, customized training at user work sites, and post-implementation operational support.

The CAMS project has served as a catalyst for redesigning administrative processes throughout Commerce. CAMS has provided managerial visibility to the processes and procedures across the Department's administrative silos and stovepipes. The Department embarked on the CAMS project, in large measure, because it realized that its financial management and other administrative processes and systems were inadequate. The CAMS project ensures that the Department has both new systems software and redesigned business processes to match. Identification and documentation of requirements for financial management and other administrative services, at the outset, heightened awareness of existing work processes. The implementation strategy included definition of an implementation model that assumed significant changes including, for example, greater standardization of processes across all operating units. Exposure to new software during testing and implementation planning prompted changes in work processes and opportunities for others. Implementation even in the early stages produced major changes. For example, when Census implemented the Core Financial Systems Cost Management Module (cost allocation and accumulation), it completely revamped its methods for distributing overhead charges among program units.

Long Development History
The objectives of the CAMS project were to replace or integrate existing financial and administrative management systems with systems that use modern technologies and operational strategies, and to provide for the maintenance of those systems as CAMS was deployed. Though these objectives were achieved, the CAMS deployment was not without its problems. CAMS has had a long development history, including several significant course corrections. Though the CAMS software was originally a COTS product, it has been modified to the point of no longer being COTS. The Department of Commerce, with contractor support, took on the role of system developer and essentially serves as the software vendor.

In the mid-1990s, the CFO and the CITRB recognized that the CAMS development was off course. A contractor was hired to perform an analysis of CAMS development and provide advice regarding the future. The CFO and CITRB, considering the contractor's recommendations, decided to retain CAMS but change the original all-in-one design to the current architecture of a core financial system, feeder systems, and data warehouse. It was deemed more costly and risky to start again with a true COTS product.

At OMBs request, in May 1999, NOAA and the Department of Commerce Office of Financial Management conducted an exhaustive evaluation of an alternative to have the Department of Interior provide cross-servicing of their COTS-based financial management system. Continuing with CAMS implementation at NOAA was judged to be the better alternative based on schedule, cost, technology, and implementation risks.

The CAMS project is undergoing a thorough analysis during the spring and summer of 2004, leading to a significant investment decision point in the fall of 2004. Meanwhile, OMB is moving forward with its Financial Management Line of Business (FM LOB) initiative, looking to provide a Government-wide solution to financial management. The useful lifetime of CAMS will be determined in the context of when the Department will migrate to one of the new OMB-sponsored FM LOB systems.

A key issue to assess is the architecture of any new financial system. The CAMS architecture with a core financial system and feeder, data warehouse, and dashboard systems was made before integrated products provided by major ERP vendors became more robust. Some feel that 'this best-of-breed strategy [was] developed in the days when various ERP software vendors had built reputations on their strengths and weaknesses' (Robb, 2004) and that a more comprehensive strategy is possible now. Others feel that the jury is still out on the effectiveness of one-stop shopping for ERPs in Federal agencies; successes have not been firmly documented.

Project Management
The Department of Commerce in recent years has recognized the need for strong project management. As such, the Department is moving forward with several activities to ensure that it has a strong project management expertise. These include project manager training; CITRB evaluation of project manager resumes; formal validation of project manager credentials; and regular, systematic Earned Value Management (EVM) analysis for IT investments under development.

The CAMS central project management team, as well as those at Census, NOAA, and NIST, are exemplars in project management to others within the Department. Though the CAMS project now has a strong project management leadership and expertise as well as a defined management structure, supported by contractors, the development of this expertise took time and hard work, benefitting from lessons learned over the duration of the project. The project management structure was a significant area of concern when course corrections were exercised in the 1990s.

Much as the overall financial management at the Department benefits from the CAMS dashboard, the dashboard concept was employed to significant advantage in the deployment of CAMS at the separate installations. These dashboards were presented to the CITRB and were instrumental in the CITRB assessment of CAMS project management and system deployment progress.

CAMS provides much of the core data that are needed for all departmental IT project managers to use in earned value management analysis of their IT investments. Following on the Department-wide initiative to use EVM and in a continuing effort to manage the CAMS project effectively, the CAMS project itself will soon be subject to EVM analysis.

Other ERP at The Department of Commerce
The Department has a number of other ERP efforts under way, with those in human resources management, acquisition, and grants management the most advanced. Some components are already feeder systems to CAMS. All of these will be affected by the Government-wide E-Government and Lines of Business initiatives. The Government-wide Recruitment One-Stop, E-Training, E-Clearance, E-Payroll, and Enterprise Human Resources Integration E-Government initiatives were originally conceived as separate E-Government initiatives but will now be rolled into a single Human Resources Management LOB. The Integrated Acquisition Environment is an E-Government initiative with multiple components addressing acquisition needs. The Grants Management LOB will be merged into Grants.gov E-Government initiative. How these will impact the Department and in what time frame is not yet clear, but ERP at the Department of Commerce and all Federal agencies will be affected in some way.

Summary Comments

Development and deployment of ERP systems at the Department of Commerce is influenced by multiple factors, which can be grouped in three broad categories: Government-wide factors, Department-specific characteristics, and challenges faced by project managers of any ERP system. Government-wide factors include Federal legislation and guidance; oversight by the Office of Management and Budget, the General Accountability Office, and others; and the President's Management agenda, including the Federal Enterprise Architecture, and E-Government and Lines of Business initiatives.

These forces provide both benefits and challenges to ERP deployment and are largely unique to the Federal environment. The Department's diversity affects how it addresses IT management. The Department of Commerce takes a federated approach, allowing each operating unit to develop its own mission systems but moving toward enterprise-wide systems for administrative activities. Because of its decentralized structure and culture, building acceptance for enterprise-wide systems is a particular challenge at the Department. General challenges affecting any ERP implementation include establishing strong project management, instituting internal process changes, and addressing technology refreshment.

BIBLIOGRAPHY

Executive Office of the President, Office of Management and Budget, The Official Web Site of the President's E-Government Initiatives, Presidential Initiatives, http://www.whitehouse.gov/omb/egov/index2.html.

Executive Office of the President, Office of Management and Budget, The Official Web Site of the President's E-Government Initiatives, Presidential Initiatives, Internal Efficiency and Effectiveness, http://www.whitehouse.gov/omb/egov/internal.htm.

Hardy, Michael, 'Commerce tests reports portal,' Federal Computer Week, 21 April, 2003.

Hardy, Michael, 'Tibco goes for fed business,' Federal Computer Week, 12 May, 2004.

Jackson, Joab, 'Tools for data-drive management,' Government Computer News, 19 July, 2004, Vol. 23, No. 19.

Joch, Alan, 'Saving time by sharing data,' Federal Computer Week, 15 March, 2004.

Robb, Karen, 'Agencywide software systems face hurdles,' Federal Times, 19 July, 2004.

US Department of Commerce, Capital Planning and Investment Control Process, September 2004, http://www.osec.doc.gov/cio/oipr/cpicprocess.htm.

US Department of Commerce, Commerce Administrative Management System, Capital Asset Plan and Business Case, September 2004.

US Department of Commerce, Enterprise Information Technology Architecture, September 2004.

US Department of Commerce, Strategic Information Technology Plan for 2004-2008, http://www.osec.doc.gov/cio/oipr/sitp.pdf.

3. Change Management in the Canadian Forces: Land Force Atlantic Area Headquarters

Lt. Col. Robert Russell

'I hope and pray that I will not have to face such a process again'.

LFAA survey respondent

INTRODUCTION

Invariably, organizational change models are founded on principles of leadership, vision, planning, communicating, and training. These are sound and enduring principles, yet insufficient in themselves to manage corporate change during the implementation of large ERP systems. Implicit in a standard software implementation is a fundamental change of business processes. In this, the scope of change is enterprise wide and of greater consequence than just new reporting lines. Change is complex, integrated, and inextricably embedded in all operational and technical aspects of the organization. It is axiomatic that the consequences of such change on an organization's human resources can be significant. Therefore, integrating processes across horizontal and vertical chains demands an integrated and structured methodology that manages human resources change to the same detail as the overall technical implementation. Failure to address change management to this degree can result in lasting and detrimental effects embedding themselves in an organization's workforce.

No one organization is immune from the all too often negative issues of organizational change. Public sector organizations are as susceptible to the adverse affects of poorly managed change as are private sector companies. The public sector also includes the less often thought of federal organizations found in the Department of Defense. They too, are prone to the adverse consequences of inadequate change management. Indeed, organizational changes within Land Force Atlantic Area Headquarters (LFAAHQ) a regional defense headquarters responsible for Army operations in the Atlantic Provinces serves as a limited but revealing study of public sector critical change management issues. Created in 1992, in Halifax, Nova Scotia with personnel strength of 212, LFAAHQ then controlled 23 subordinate organizations throughout New Brunswick, Nova Scotia, Prince Edward Island, and Newfoundland and Labrador. In the years between 1994 and 2001, the HQ was subjected to the introduction of new enterprise resource planning (ERP) systems (for human resources and financial management), new business planning and performance measurement systems, structural reorganizations, and personnel reductions. A survey of the HQ's employees following the implementation of these initiatives revealed a failure to fully appreciate and manage change. The end result had a lasting impact on the HQ.

The goal of the LFAA survey was to determine what public sector employees considered important to maintain the well being of both an organization and its employees during periods of change. This premise of the study was that change could have sweeping and lasting effects on an organization. The preponderance of historical studies had indicated that these effects are negative. Therefore, it is in the interest of an organization to implement organizational change in a manner that maintains the well being of the organization and its employees. However, the aspects that contribute to the successful implementation of change are not always known, understood, or addressed by an organization during periods of organizational change. This was found to be the case in LFAA. This paper is a brief discussion of central change management issues that were reinforced by the results of the survey, and serve as a useful reminder of the critical issues of change management that must be addressed, regardless of organization.

'The process must be out in the open'.

LFAA survey respondent

STRATEGY OF CHANGE

There is a great deal of discussion on the strategies of implementing organizational change initiatives. Many diverse models of change management are available. What is important to note is that an 'either/or' approach to organizational change need not be used. Rather, using aspects (i.e. the relevant practices) of several processes or models may be more suitable than employing a single approach or model. Indeed, under the umbrella of a large organizational change, different processes can accommodate different organizational objectives. Often, these may be short lived and employed only in limited time frames. In other words, enterprise wide change is complex and far-reaching. Components of the overall change may demand specific methodologies to be used for specific durations. Often, these microcosms may also appear to conflict with the overall orientation of the enterprise change model. It is important that the intent and expectations of these short-term methods be clearly communicated to the employees.

What is most important is that whichever approach is decided upon in a time of such difficult and broad transition simplicity is sought. As such, the management of change needs a tangible construct to allow for visibility, transparency, forward thinking, decision-making, analyses, familiarity, and comfort. Proactive and continuous change management needs an open, transparent model that pulls together all aspects of the enterprise wide change that is easily and effectively communicated.

Change management strategies associated with an ERP implementation should be introduced, controlled, and implemented similar to the activities of the technical implementation. Dealing with issues of changes early, and defining them clearly during strategy development will lend itself more readily to introducing change incrementally. For example, change has to be linked to the overarching goal of the implementation – the 'why?'". If an organization's goal is innovation, it has to be understood that innovation is different than efficiency as it is different than cost savings. Importantly, these goals all require different changes in your human resources so they are aligned to the new system. Identifying these changes must be done in the early planning phase, so that the change control mechanism that one employs can be aligned to the overall implementation of change and the organization's goals.

Using such a basic and sound implementation process (or similar methodology) simplifies the means to track, assess and refine changes proactively and timely, yet before they are introduced to the broad population of a company. It is a controlling structure that is needed to corral the integrated, empowered, and collaborative teams' mindsets, decisions, and other changes to ensure that they support the intent of the technical implementation. In the end, an audit trail of how and why changes occurred will be created that can be reviewed and adjusted as necessary. Equally important is that throughout the implementation of change, change strategies must also be linked to existing and ongoing organizational plans, such as a human resources plan, to ensure normal operations. For example, is the impact of a change (such as reorganization) minimized to allow for normal career progression, training and development?

What was found to be significant in LFAA's circumstances is that throughout the period of 1996 to 2001, considerable energy and associated staff checks were conducted focusing on structural reorganizations, changed processes, the reduction of personnel, and the division of responsibilities among the remaining employees. In short, who was to do what, with how many personnel, and to whom do they report? At no point during any of these changes was there a change management strategy that maintained the critical functions that keep the organization's human resources cohesive during the process of change itself. Little thought was given to addressing the consequences of organizational change (beyond resource savings). With technical goals being the primary objective, minimal consideration was given to potential employee resistance to change, or to the potential disruption to embedded organizational cultures. The consequences were dire. The absence of a sound change model contributed to the lack of clarity in the overall process, negatively affected communication and senior endorsement, confused the metrics of progress and decision-making, and disrupted the overall comfort of employees. The resulting employee assessment of the implementation of those changes was negative, and the process noted to be 'largely dysfunctional' (Ryder, 1999).

'The organization is more than an empty structure.'

LFAA survey respondent

The Effect of Organizational Culture

In this regard, LFAA was slightly different than much of the research literature of the time. In general, previous studies had noted that the overall successes of change strategies can be influenced by an organization's culture, perhaps even by an organization's sub-cultures. Schein (1992) discussed reengineering efforts in the face of organizational culture. He suggested that sustaining any change required first altering an organization's culture. This is no small task. Beckhard and Pritchard (1992) suggested that such a cultural change may require setting up 'supporting educational activities'. This also means dealing with long-term employees. Generally, those that have been longest in a company will harbor the most resentment for change (O'Neil and Lenn, 1995). Interestingly, Schein noted that change breaks the implicit contract between management and employees, and, therefore risks undermining management credibility. Perhaps this is no different than the predicament that change causes vis a vis psychological contract violations. This was reinforced by Robinson and Rousseau (1994, p. 258,) who argued that employees will be unwilling to support change, or in fact even remain with an organization, if managers ignore the perceived mutual obligations that define the employee management relationship. This is particularly so in times of wholesale organizational change, when employees are most likely to be sensitive to management's actions. They noted that a challenge for management will be, 'to keep changes in employment conditions from becoming violations'. Mone (1997, p. 317) more ominously warned that much of the new literature on the psychological contract found in organizations urges employees to be 'self starters' and 'not to be committed to the organization because it cannot commit to you'.

In LFAA however, despite a wide variety of respondents (i.e. uniformed, civilian, contractors, male, female, old, and young) there were no strong opinions regarding statements about organizational culture. Further, most were neutral on the organization and its relationships. The majority of employees liked their job and felt a responsibility to continue in their position. Perhaps there is greater security in public sector organizations, and more allegiance to the organization and its mission, and less the position. It is unknown if this is an accurate statement. LFAA was not a widely diversified culture. Consequently, it was still felt that there is a continuous need to explore differences among the varied segments of the workforce. Such differences are easily recognized as potential points of friction. Perhaps however, they are not so readily recognized as the root causes that could ultimately dishevel a process of change. This suggestion was somewhat noticeable in differences of opinions (in LFAA) during the actual implementation of change. This issue could be critical for more diversified organizations that may have employees from a variety of cultural and social backgrounds. Such organizations must be particularly aware of this risk.

'Pick a manager who is trustworthy.'

LFAA survey respondent

Management of Change

The method by which strategy formulation for change is developed, executed, and managed can negatively impact its implementation. Often, reorganization activities are at least initially centralized amongst senior staff. Generally, this is in effort to avoid rumors, panic, and internal turmoil. The perception of fairness and balance is important here, and there are a number of significant factors reinforced in the LFAA study for management to consider.

It is not only the strategy of implementing change that is important to the process, but also that those managers that will implement it are equally critical. First, effective communication of the strategy and timely buy-in by middle management is important in order to win their commitment (O'Neil and Lenn, 1995). O'Neil and Lenn suggested that a major cause of inconsistent results in organizational changes is middle management's failure to understand and endorse corporate efforts. It is thought that this is because their interest in the implementation efforts is dependent on their enthusiasm for the overall strategy. It is an understatement to note that management is important to the change process. They are the ones who implement change in an environment that usually becomes very challenging.

Within LFAA, employees were inclined to feel that reorganization activities were influenced negatively by rank (levels of management), and that they were less inclined to completely trust their supervisors to complete a reorganization of the unit. It is unknown if this was completely an issue of trust, competency, hidden agendas, or lack of training amongst managers. Training was the only issue of these that was confirmed. Almost all employees believed that staff responsible for change efforts should have received specialized training prior to commencing their work.

In the absence of training, an alternative was felt to be the use of contractors. LFAA respondents were, however, split on the use of third parties (contracted agencies) to assist in changes. In general, many felt that, 'the money was spent to no avail. They [consultants] had to listen [to employees] in the end anyway'. Given this view however, civilians were more inclined to third party consultants than were their military counterparts. Significant relationships were also noted suggesting that supervisors and females also believed there was a need for consultants. Uniformed personnel stood alone in this area.

Miles et al. (1995) identified three factors necessary for successful organizational redesign: change must be essential; it must be accompanied by a clear vision and process; and importantly, it must have a supporting management philosophy. Arguably, the most important tool for any organizational change is ensuring that a vision statement is articulated. It is essential that this statement is understood and clearly communicated to everyone in the organization, be supported at all management levels, and be devoid of platitudes. There is little surprise that the majority of LFAA believed in the value of a communications plan. During implementation, most preferred to receive information from their supervisors and they were far less desirous of receiving information from impersonal resources (i.e. intranet). Without question, employees wanted a more personal touch when dealing with the organization.

Communication was indeed a major issue, and remains a critical component of any strategy. Often however, communication is undertaken, but it is incomplete or erroneous (Wagar, 1996). In a study of 531 organizations undergoing major restructuring, Larkin and Larkin (1996) asked CEOs, 'If you could go back and change one thing, what would it be?' The most frequent response was 'the way I communicated with my employees'. Their advice was: communicate facts not values; do it face to face; and target front line supervisors rather than letting executives introduce the changes. This advice is supported by experiences in LFAA. Most noted the critical importance of clearly articulating objectives and milestones, ensuring an understanding of how the process will work, what areas will be affected, and what the end-state should look like. Many noted that they were never told of the reason for changes in the first place. It can not be repeated enough – the lack of effective communication leads to misinformation and misunderstanding. In turn, this creates discourse even amongst managers that leads to second-guessing strategies (O'Neil and Lenn, 1995).

The effects of change must be balanced equally, even amongst levels of management. Within LFAA, the majority of all employees believed it necessary to have an equitable restructuring process that affected all hierarchical levels of the organization. Even though this means changing managers. As noted by O'Neil and Lenn (1995. p. 31), 'research on firms undergoing turnaround strategies gives some credence to the belief that a firm cannot reverse its performance without the replacement of its top manager. According to these researchers, [the manager's] knowledge base may not fit the new environment'. Leatt and Baker (1997) noted that reengineering requires changing people.

Interchanging managers can happen not only after organizational change, but perhaps for the implementation of change itself. Although LFAA did not have sufficient resources, perhaps there could have been cause to employ different managers. Armstrong-Stassen (1998) argued that those managers that were optimistic, had a high future success expectancy and a high tolerance for ambiguity, were less negatively affected by downsizing than those who lacked these attributes. Without a doubt, employees within LFAA were susceptible to the existing attitudes of those who implemented change. Unfortunately, many noted the period to be one of significant anxiety, stress, and loss of morale.

It was suggested during one of the change initiatives that the intended organizational end-state did not resemble the actual end-state. How many reorganizations and consequently personnel are affected by such mid-implementation changes? Often different levels of the hierarchy may not even share the same understanding of the intended changes to begin with. Indeed, senior management perspectives on the planning, implementation, and outcomes associated with preparing an organization for change may differ from an employee's perspective. Thus, it is necessary to ensure that viewpoints by management are not inherently different from the remainder of an organization's employees. An effective method for controlling such risks is allowing for plans for change to be designed from the bottom up, but implemented from the top down. This process was effectively used in a reorganization of LFAA's Combat Training Centre (subsequent to this study). The reorganization plan and the implementation of changes were formulated with the direct involvement of affected personnel in a large coordinated working group format. The plan was designed so that a trial period of six months was built into the implementation. The temporary reorganization was then assessed, allowing for changes to the final organization prior to its final implementation. This dual approach helped generate a number of innovations that would not have been possible through a one-sided approach. The point is that effective planning is critical, but it must strike the right balance of employee input and management guidance.

'The old way was abandoned too quickly'.

LFAA survey respondent

Implementation of Change

There is a substantial body of literature addressing the important tactics of change implementation. Several points were found to be important to the employees of LFAA.

The majority of personnel in LFAA felt it was necessary to be actively involved in any reorganization that their organization was undertaking. A significant positive relationship existed between the respondent's experience, component, and gender and the degree of employee involvement. This relationship suggested that females and military respondents believed that employee involvement was important. Of those groups that felt involvement was not warranted, it was generally believed it was because they had not participated in reorganization before. Ironically, the more participative the process that is used, which studies purport to be essential to success (Tang and Fuller, 1995), the harder change initiatives such as downsizing can became. One respondent of O'Neil and Lenn (1995) suggested that management levels that participated in downsizing should be replaced, '[downsizes] don't have the ability or energy to get the staffs productivity up again - this guy's been downsizing for ten years, now we have to start building, is he really the person we want?' It is apparent that the experience of downsizing has a profound and lasting effect on management. Wright and Darling (1998) interviewed ten executives from both public and private sector organizations across Canada who had participated in downsizing. Their interviews revealed downsizers to be negatively affected by their activities. The scope of these effects was striking, and included the impact on family. One executive described how the experience 'still haunted her after ten years'. This reinforces an earlier point on changing managers.

The majority of personnel in the HQ felt that changes should have been preceded by a survey of existing efficiencies so that comparable data was available to determine the final outcome of the results of change. Further, they believed that changes to the organization should not be considered complete until a formal assessment was conducted on the initiative to determine that it had added value to the organization. Most LFAA employees also felt that in order for the reorganizations to be truly effective, restructuring needed to have been accompanied by systemic changes to the organization. This is in addition to changes in process and work practices. Those who were affected by the changes wanted to ensure that it was substantive, and was going to be value added. In colloquial terms, the change had to be worth the pain.

Although the overall approach and view of an implementation can be holistic, the implementation of change should be conducted incrementally – thus creating an iteration – that can be analyzed and tested before further forward movement is made. Analogous to engineering implementations, bugs, defects, and other integration issues can be captured early. Issues can then be resolved while still relatively minor. And changes could also be released in a measured manner. For example, the final phase of an implementation is not the time for system introduction, training, and user acceptance tests. There is change implicit in all of these areas. Equally, just prior to going live, is not the time to discover that significant change management issues exist. This view was reiterated throughout LFAA's analysis, 'Do the changes in increments if possible. Give the change time to adjust before moving on. Stay flexible, as the situation changes you may want to re-visit original plans to see whether the next step is the best course of action. Have an evaluation period after the changes are made to see if further [change] is required'.

'The employees made it work'.

LFAA survey respondent

The Change in Human Resources

The impact of change in an organization is significant, and the consequences are at times unexpected. During wholesale organizational changes, one must prepare for unforeseen personnel reductions. Given the negative consequences associated with many organizational changes, none suggested that some individuals may leave organizations as a means of 'ego-protection, or self serving defensiveness to avert the cause of dissatisfaction and seek escape'. An often and unexpected cause of such a departure of employees is the 'cesspool syndrome', where the most qualified personnel have chosen to voluntarily leave an organization, leaving less qualified employees the opportunity to rise to more senior positions (Burke and Nelson, 1998). It was abundantly clear from the view of those that remained at LFAA during the period of organizational changes that, good people left the organization when they were needed most.

Equally, the requirement for organizational efficiencies or restructuring could lead to directed reductions. In December 1994, the Management, Command and Control Re-engineering Team was created with the explicit intent of overseeing the reorganization and reduction of HQ personnel throughout the Canadian Forces by fifty percent. Given this direction, should reductions be targeted or be across the board cuts? Should management equally be reduced? Are there innocent victims? For example, across the board cuts, although perceived as being fair, tend to penalize efficient parts of an organization, and may not necessarily be linked to the strategic priorities of the organization. In delayering, management is seen as absorbing their fair share of cuts. However, the remaining management levels often absorb the workload, and perhaps without the benefit of the necessary experience or training. Further, who implements long-term changes and manages the organization at the same time? And, at the end of it all, what continuity is left? In the end, what is equitable must have been previously determined. And the strategic objectives must be adhered to so that the long-term consequences remain positive.

Non-prioritized downsizing (across the board) was perceived as a negative approach in the Canadian Forces. It was, as Cameron (1994) noted, 'like tossing a grenade into a crowded room'. There was little anticipation of the effects that an early Force Reduction Plan (early retirement incentive) would have. Applicants for this program far exceeded the number of releases that were originally sought. Many applicants had to be denied in order to retain existing capabilities. Many who were accepted for early release were among the best employees. Others were persons who were left on strength too long poisoning the work environment. Subsequent to this approach, the Department of Defense embarked on a complete occupational review, and it now targeted select positions in accordance with the strategic direction enforced. However, it has been a process of trial and error, and has been unduly influenced by changes in both strategic direction, and budgetary realities.

After major changes, an organization still has to contend with the results of its initiatives. In this, attitudes among survivors can be hostile. Many if not all employees will be affected by survivor's syndrome. In LFAA, those that remained have received little more than increased workloads, broader responsibilities, no additional compensation, and a host of other negative consequences (i.e. decreased loyalties, lower morale). Unfortunately, there was no increase in training and development opportunities. Moreover, changes to the human resources management system did not effectively recognize the changes in the reduced force. An organization also has to question; if a contingency strategy for failure to adopt a new organization system must be developed. The costs of failure are dramatic, not only financially but also in terms of the mental and physical health of employees (Tang and Fuller, 1995).

Implications of the Study

A number of implications were drawn from the LFAA study. First, there are several activities that an organization should undertake prior to commencing any reorganization process. Personnel responsible for organizational changes must be trained in change management activities. It is likely that such training will increase the amount of trust in both the process and among employees. There needs to be a clear vision of where an organization wants to be before commencing a renewal process. This vision must be articulated to all employees, with clear objectives and notions on how and when the reorganization will occur. As well, a system of performance measurement should be embraced before committing to reorganization. End state measures of costs savings, increased productivity, or efficiencies cannot be determined in the absence of a performance model. In process measuring, the reorganization must be viewed from a variety of perspectives, and not only from a broad corporate overview. The process of change will affect the many levels of an organization in different ways.

Aspects of several organizational change models or options may be more suitable than using just a single approach. However, these processes must be investigated before commencing any initiative. Most importantly, whatever process is implemented, it should all have the support of management, and be well understood by all employees. A continuous assessment of the process and its value should also be conducted. This will require a sound and aggressive communications plan and performance measurement loop that is endorsed and adhered to by senior management. Activities like downsizing, restructuring, and reorganization should be undertaken as part of the larger process of organizational change. Employees want to see fundamental and positive (value added) differences made in all work areas if their organization is going to pursue large organizational change initiatives. Achieving only technical objectives will not be satisfactory.

During implementation, differences in opinion will arise between groups over a variety of different issues. These differences can and will generate conflict between members of an organization. For example, how will management's obligations and responsibilities to their employees be affected when they are under the same threatening consequences of reorganization themselves? Factors of background, gender, age, and hierarchical position have to be accounted for. This is a critical issue. Ideally, all activities must be perceived as equitable among the various groups. Failure to make every effort to realize this will quickly lead to a breakdown of trust, morale, and well being in the organization. The employees are the critical resource that will sustain the organization during organizational change. Yet, those who are most affected by change are rarely managed well during the process of reorganization. Such human resource issues will spin off other consequences (i.e. voluntary departures) that an organization may not have anticipated.

The LFAA report also pointed to some post-reorganization implications. That is, organizations should not deviate from their core competencies after reorganization. Stability is important and organizations must continue to build on core competencies. Once an organization has undergone a fundamental change, it cannot return to the old method of conducting business. Obviously, the organizational change process must address the future methodologies of conducting business. As observed by Wahan and Green (1996), redesign must be viewed as 'starting over'. Similarly, one LFAA employee noted that if the change wasn't 'refreshing', than re-evaluation was in order. And by implication, the success of the implementation was very much in question.

CONCLUSION

Fundamental organizational changes cannot be reversed so readily if they are determined to be inappropriate to an organization's needs. And the thrust of historical studies suggests that effects of workforce changes are negative. Yet, despite this, the trend to change organizations within the public sector continues – a trend that is equally prevalent in the Department of Defense.

And in this sector's haste to implement change, little consideration is often given to the sweeping consequences of inappropriate change management. This is unfortunate – failure to understand change and its effects can have a lasting and negative impact on an organization. Thought must extend beyond just achieving the goals of technical and structural changes to addressing the important human resource issues of change. The critical human resource functions that keep an organization cohesive during and after the process of reorganization are vitally important. The management of these issues must be an early and fundamental consideration in the overall strategy of organizational change.

LFAA serves as an illustration of change management issues in the public sector. Notwithstanding the limitations of the study, the results are important. They add to the body of research that has already been conducted. Most importantly, this study involves an empirical analysis of reorganization at LFAAHQ, which has not been done before. This in itself is a major achievement, and can be used as a stepping stone for further research and examination into implementing reorganization in the Canadian Forces as it undertakes future change objectives.

BIBLIOGRAPHY

Armstrong-Stassen, M. 'Downsizing the Federal Government: A Longitudinal Study of Managers Reactions', Canadian Journal of Administrative Sciences, Vol. 15. No. 4, 1998, 310–21.

Armstrong-Stassen, M. 'Survivor's Reactions to a Workforce reduction: A Comparison of Blue-collar Workers and their Supervisors', Canadian Journal of Administrative Sciences, Vol. 10, No. 4, 1993, 334–43.

Bacharach, W. and Bamberger, S. 'The Reorganization Transformation Process: The Micropolitics of Dissonance Reduction and the Alignment of Logics of Action', Administrative Science Quarterly, Vol. 41, No. 3, 1996, 477–506.

Beckhard, R. and Pritchard, W. 'Changing the Essence: The Art of Creating and Leading Fundamental Change in Organizations', 37–48, 1992. Reprinted in Ott, J.S., 'Focusing the Effort: Crucial Themes that Drive Change,'Classic Readings in Organizational Behavior', Wadsworth Publishing Company, 1996, 513–19.

Brockner, J., DeWitt, R., Grover, S., and Reed, T. 'When is it Especially Important to explain Why: Factors Affecting the Relationship Between Manager's Expectations of a layoff and Survivors Reactions to the Layoff', Journal of Experimental Social Psychology, Vol. 26, No. 5, 1990, 389–407.

Buono, A. 'Reengineering Partnerships: Process Intervention in Strategic Alliances', S.A.M Advanced Management Journal, Vol. 62, No. 23, 1997, 21–6.

Burke, R. and Nelson, D. 'Lessons Learned', Canadian Journal of Administrative Sciences, Vol. 15, No. 4, 1998, 372–81.

Cameron, K.'Strategies for Successful Organizational Downsizing', Human Resource Management, Vol. 33, No. 2, 1994.

Cameron, K.S. and Freeman, S.J. 'Best Practices in White Collar Downsizing: Managing Contradictions', Academy of Management Executive, Vol. 5, No. 3, 1991, 57–73.

Cameron, K. 'Strategic Organizational Downsizing: An Extreme Case', Research in Organizational Behaviour, Vol. 20, 1998, 185–229.

Cascio, W.F. 'Downsizing: What Do We Know? What Have We Learned?', Academy of Management Executive, Vol. 7, No. I, 1993, 95–104.

Freeman, S. 'Organizational Downsizing as Convergence or Reorientation: Implications for Human Resource Management', Human Resource Management, Vol. 33, No. 2, 1994.

Greer, C.R., Youngblood, A., and Gray, D.A. 'Human Resource Management Outsourcing: The Make or Buy Decision', Academy of Management Executive, Vol. 13, No. 3, 1999, 85–96,

Greenwood, R. 'The Reforming Organization', Administrative Science Quarterly, Vol. 41, No. 1, 1996, 181–84.

Grossman, B.A. 'Corporate Loyalty: Does it have a Future?', Journal of Business Ethics, Vol. 8, No. 7, 1989.

Haveman, H. 'Between a Rock and a Hard Place: Organizational Change and Performance Under Conditions of Fundamental Environmental Transformation', Administrative Science Quarterly, Vol. 37, No. 1, 1992.

Havlovic, S., Bouthilette, F., and van der Wal, R. 'Coping With Downsizing and Job Loss: Lessons from the Shaughnessy Hospital Closure', Canadian Journal of Administrative Sciences, Vol. 15, No. 4, 1998, 322–32.

Ivancevich, J. and Donnelly, J. 'Relation of Organizational Structure to Job Satisfaction, Anxiety-Stress, and Performance', Administrative Science Quarterly, Vol. 20, 1975, 272–80.

Koys, D. and Armacost, R. 'Organizational Resizing and Human Resource Management', SAM Advanced Management Journal, Vol. 55, No. 3, 1990.

Larkin, T.J. and Larkin, S. 'Reaching and Changing Front-line Employees', Harvard Business Review, Vol. 74, No. 3, 1996, 95–104.

Leanna, C. and Feldman, D. 'Better Practices in Managing Layoffs', Human Resource Management, Vol. 33, No. 2, 1994.

Leatt, P. and Baker, R. 'Downsizing, Reengineering and Restructuring: Long Term Implications for Healthcare Organizations', Frontiers of Health Services Management, Vol. 13, Iss. 4, 1997, 3–17.

Lippet, R. 'Humane Downsizing: Organizational Renewal Versus Organizational Depression', SAM Advanced Management Journal, Vol. 49, No. 3, 1984.

Mackay, J.M. 'Behavioural and Attitudinal Effects of Layoffs on Survivor Employees in two Nova Scotia Firms', Management Research Project, Saint Mary's University, April 1992.

Mackenzie, H. 'Behavioural and Attitudinal Effects of Layoffs on Survivor Employees', Management Research Project, Saint Mary's University, April 1996.

MacKillop. M. 'Avoid Showdown When Seeking to Relocate Staff', The Globe and Mail, 15 November, 1999, M-1.

McKinley, W. 'How to Tame the Diversified Firm', Administrative Sciences Quarterly, Vol. 42, No. I, 1997, 191–95.

Miles, R., Coleman, H., and Creed, W. 'Keys to Success in Corporate Redesign', California Management Review, Vol. 37, No. 3, 1995.

Mone, M. 'How we got Along after Downsizing: Post Downsizing Trust as a Double-Edged Sword', Public Administration Quarterly, Vol. 21, No. 3, 1997, 309–36.

Murray, T.J. 'For Downsizers, the Real Misery is Yet to Come', Business Month, Vol. 133, February 1989, 71–2.

O'Neil, H. and Lenn, D.J. 'Voices of Survivors: Words That Downsizing CEOs Should Hear', Academy of Management Executive, Vol. 9, No. 4, 1995, 23–34.

Rama, M. 'Efficient Public Sector Downsizing', Finance and Development, Vol. 34, No. 3, 1997, 40–3.

Robinson, S. and Rousseau, D. 'Violating the Psychological Contract: Not the Exception but the Norm', Journal of Organizational Behavior, Vol. 15, 1994, 245–59.

Ryder, L.H. 'Effects of Downsizing on Survivors Attitudes and Behavior Towards Work', Management Research Project, Saint Mary's University, April 1999.

Schappi, J. Ed. 'Grievance Guide', The Bureau of National Affairs, 1983.

Schein, E. 'Organizational Culture and Leadership', 374–92, 1992. Reprinted in Otto, J.S. 'The Learning Leader as Culture Manager', Classic Readings in Organizational Behavior, Wadsworth Publishing Company, 1996, 228–37.

Sparrow, P. and Cooper, C. 'New Organizational Forms: The Strategic Relevance of Future Psychological Contract Scenarios', Canadian Journal of Administrative Sciences, Vol. 15, No.4, 1998, 356–71.

Tang, T.L. and Fuller, R.M. 'Corporate Downsizing: What Managers can do to Lessen the Negative Effects of Layoffs', SAM Advanced Management Journal, Vol. 60, No. 4, 1995.

Wagar, T.H. 'Exploring the Consequences of Workforce Reduction', Canadian Journal of Administrative Sciences, Vol. 15, No. 4, 1998, 300–08.

Wagar, T.H. 'Factors Affecting Permanent Workforce Reduction', Canadian Journal of Administrative Sciences, Vol. 14, No. 3, 1997, 303–14.

Wagar, T.H. 'What do we Know About Downsizing?', Benefits and Pension Monitor, June 1996, 19–69.

Wahan, V. and Green, B. 'Viewpoint Reengineering: Clarifying the Confusion', SAM Advanced Management Journal, Vol. 61, No. 3, 1996.

Wright, B. and Darling, J. 'The Executioner's Song: Listening to Downsizer's Experiences', Canadian Journal of Administrative Sciences, Vol. 15, No. 4, 1998, 339–55.

4. Emerging Doctrines of Government Performance and Federal ERP Change Management

Daniel L. Cuda

INTRODUCTION

Theoretically, enterprise resource planning (ERP) in the Federal Government promises new opportunities for improving its performance management. Specifically, this means managing government business operations within the context of measurable outcomes and results. To achieve this, managers need reliable, verifiable, consistently defined information. For this, in turn, they need an ERP's comprehensive, synthesized representation of the overall activity. In this ideal state, the formerly stove-piped resource management systems of personnel, logistics, and finance will be integrated with information on organizational outcomes to create a comprehensive, process-centered representation of the government enterprise.

It is a long way to this idealized state of affairs. But improvements in these areas have been ongoing over several presidencies. The Bush Administration, beginning in 2001, continued these trends and initiated a new round of government-wide initiatives seeking greater budget and performance integration. In framing its effort, the initiative notes, 'Managers do not have timely and complete information with which to monitor and improve their results'.[1] It continues, 'There is little reward, in budgets or in compensation, for running programs efficiently. And once money is allocated to program, there is no requirement to revisit the question of whether the results obtained are solving problems the American people care about'.[2]

Despite these admirable goals and the emerging potential for change, there is reason to be pessimistic. The Federal Government is enormous and complex. Its largest single organization, the Department of Defense is by itself the largest operating enterprise in the world, the nation's largest employer, and first on the Fortune 500 if its budgets are equated with revenue. Putting aside the President's hundred-fold greater task of governing the executive branch, some have thought the job of Secretary of Defense (by itself) was beyond human accomplishment. The celebrated management analyst Peter Drucker offered the opinion, 'I am not yet convinced that the job of Secretary of Defense of the United States is really possible (although I admit I cannot conceive of an alternative)'.[3] Drucker is not alone. Eliot Cohen, a respected academic and commentator on defense issues, starts with Drucker's comment and writes, 'The truth is that being secretary of defense is an impossible job – if one hopes to change quickly the institutions of the armed forces rather than merely preside over them'.[4]

To actually do more than preside, the President, the Secretary of Defense, or any agency head, needs integrated information to manage their enterprise. But this is exactly the problem in the DoD and throughout the Federal Government. At the center of the problem is its limited ability to link budget and execution information with its performance and functional management systems. The retired chair of Goldman, Sachs & Co., Walter Friedman, conducted a survey of the DoD financial system in 2001 at the request of the Secretary of Defense. At the completion of the study Friedman summarized the problem: 'DoDs financial infrastructure was not set up to run an enterprise of remotely this complexity. DoDs financial architecture essentially consists of numerous feeder systems which feed information up to core accounting systems. They were originally designed to perform purposes in the stovepipes or areas in which they were set up, they were not designed to speak to the systems higher up'.[5] From Friedman's comments, it is clear the need for ERP exists in the DoD and throughout the government. But as is well known, need alone will not bring about change. The opportunities to muddle through are too frequent and money flows too freely to make the need so plain that change occurs without effort. This is the challenge of change management – to bring about change before crisis makes it clear to all what needs to be done. Among the many factors needed for change management, there needs to be a vision.

Vision is a key element of change management. When it can be communicated, and moves beyond the intuition of the central decision maker, it can become the touchstone for managing change. Vision constitutes the place to be arrived at, the destination of the journey, and the justification for the pain of change. To communicate this destination and plant the vision in the persons who must bring it to reality, something tangible and concrete is most likely to quickly communicate. Consider the role of vision within a group embarked on an overland trek. It could be the story of a biblical wandering in the desert or a wagon train settling the American West. Metaphorically, vision is the identification of an end place: the object of the journey. The identification of a distant mountain pass on the horizon can certainly intimidate with its remoteness and difficulty, but it constitutes a reference that communicates what needs to be done with every new step. Successfully formulated, communicated, and internalized, and without a great many words, vision can guide activity down to a fine level of detail. In general, not all change activities will be blessed with or may even need the grand peak on the horizon. But the fundamental abstraction of vision is its ability to guide subordinate activity; to provide a sense of what is good and desirable and to make concrete that which is to be avoided.

CHANGE MANAGEMENT IN THE PUBLIC SECTOR

Many have noted the absence of profit in the public sector as a fundamental difference from the private. The simple guidance to 'spend less, sell more' that leads to private sector profits can be viewed as a vision of sorts. It can provide that fundamental guidance throughout the enterprise that is nearly applicable to any part of the organization and tells managers on any given morning what their priorities should be. As many have noted, the public sector lacks this overarching formula that can animate the daily work of the public manager. Again, the basic question for both public and private sectors remains: What should be done? What is good for my organization (and implicitly for me) and what should be avoided? Private sector managers have a more ready answer to these questions. The public sector manager has a more difficult task, and one that is all the more difficult when he or she is required to lead change.

This chapter offers one possibility for constituting a vision for public sector performance to aid the activities of change management. It focuses on an element of the Federal Government that may most likely correspond to the distant mountain as a shared destination for federal ERP. That element is the real, tangible, and authoritative guidance provided by federal statutes – specifically the collective ideas for Federal Government performance that have placed within the statutes over the last two decades. For almost a century, efficiency was a primary objective of government management,[6] but now this narrow performance paradigm has been broken and new concepts are emerging. These developments include the creation of formal government accounting standards, the requirements for agencies to link their activities with specified outputs and outcomes, and the production of auditable financial reports. The Government Performance and Results Act of 1993 is the most famous member of this group, but there is a larger set of lesser-known statutes that are slowly changing the face of the Federal Government and may collectively constitute a vision of public sector performance.

Statutes are long-term permanent influences on the future of the federal enterprise. They constitute permanent influences that shape the form and purpose of government in the same way climate shapes the natural world. For this reason they are more suitable for building the vision behind ERP implementation. The fundamental reason is that ERP implementation will not be the work of any single Presidential administration, any single cabinet secretary, nor any transient assistant secretary. It will be implemented by the much-maligned civil service of the Federal Government: the permanent officers of government who toil on its behalf through inaugurations, confirmations, and election. For better or for worse, these are the managers who are the objects of change management and who must take the steps to get to that distant vision of federal ERP.

The statutes represent a more-permanent set of governmental influences than the collective preferences that come and go with presidential administration. Neither do statutes represent the preferences of those honorable individuals appointed with the advice and consent of the Senate, whose transient preferences are often endured and sometimes ignored by government managers. After all, the average tenure of Senate confirmed personnel within the Federal Government is said to be less than thirty months. In this group we can include all the members of the federal 'Plum Book'. These are the senior civilians appointed in conjunction with any new administration that may not require Senatorial confirmation, but instead typically fill out the deputy assistant secretary positions within administration and constitute the action officers for the more senior Senate-confirmed positions. Altogether, these individuals will be gone no later than when the executive branch changes party control, and probably as early as when personally undertaken initiatives fail to make suitable progress. Taken together, the permanent officers of government can perhaps be forgiven for looking on their appointed leadership as transients. In the course of a professional life they may be seen as constituting little more than seasonal issues.

But this view of the permanent structure of executive branch government does not automatically lead to the cynic's conclusion that the federal bureaucracy is self-serving and corrupt. Rather what can be said is that the permanent members of the Senior Executive Service and the supporting senior General Service (GS) positions, first of all have a noticeably longer-term view of the government enterprise than their transient leadership. We should also include within this group field grade and flag rank military officers. Not to be inappropriately uncritical, all these groups have a long-term view of their personal career paths and of the trouble that can be gained by too easily succumbing to the unbridled enthusiasms of every new administration and its revolving set of personnel. But aside from these particular characteristics, a feature that is probably true of any group, this chapter will proceed on the assumption that where possible, these permanent officers of government will seek to improve the services and performance of the executive branch whenever they are offered a real opportunity. Consistent with their own professional time-horizons, what they seek is a more permanent guide for their long-term role in the implementation of public sector ERP.

Why focus on statute as a basis for vision? The written law, and its underpinning logic, constitutes the least changeable and most fixed point of navigation for the government enterprise. For this reason, statutory doctrine (the written law and the intent behind it) is an important element of the vision necessary for change management. A statutory doctrine is the definable theme in a swath of legislation that constitutes guidance from the political side of government. Under most circumstances these doctrines carry with them the deepest legitimacy within the ranks of career government officers. They become the 'trump' of policy debates whose invocation can settle issues and dissolve opposition. For them, they move beyond the too-frequent invocation of 'the Deputy Assistant Secretary wants' as the basis of government activity, and onto a more permanent and less changeable set of guidance that is deeply sought by those officers seeking to know what is good and desirable for their agency.

Where We Are At: Moving from Federal Government 'As-Is'

The emerging doctrines of performance management are about more than money. As will be seen the new focus is on results and outcomes. Yet the balance between the expenses of the enterprise and their related results remains at the center of the issue. Expenses are largely about the use of appropriated funds, and appropriated funds are about budgeting. For this reason, the history of public sector performance measurement is largely intertwined with the control of appropriated funds and of budgets. Despite the fundamental Constitutional requirement that, 'no money shall be drawn from the Treasury, but in consequence of appropriations made by law',[7] the modern history of fiscal control began much later. It started with the passage and subsequent amendment of the Anti-Deficiency Act (ADA) between 1868 and 1950. The intent of the act is captured within Title 31 US Code. Its fundamental tenet is the authorization of criminal penalties for the expenditure of federal funds in excess of Congressional appropriations.[8] Perhaps it is the threat of fines and imprisonment, but it is no overstatement to give the Anti-Deficiency Act a central role in the world-view of public sector comptrollers and Chief Financial Officers (CFOs).

Despite the Anti-Deficiency Act's influence within the public sector comptroller community, its role in public sector performance management is negligible. The fundamental requirements of the act are for the maintenance of expenditures within specified categories and limits. Elaborate procedures and information systems have been instituted within the federal financial community to ensure compliance with these categories and the intent of the

Anti-Deficiency Act. These information systems serve only to place limits on spending and to ensure the maintenance of spending within specified categories. They are typically unconnected with other public sector performance information systems. For example, personnel and real property management function may only be partially relatable to the budget system that theoretically offers an annual review of the overall enterprise. The overall effect is to place financial information within a unique 'stovepipe' operating in parallel with other sets of management information systems.

One long-standing critique of Federal Government management and oversight has been its fascination with the parts rather than its overall outcomes or results. This is particularly true for the management information systems that ideally would be linked with financial systems. Personnel management and the associated management information system is about placing a federal employee in a position, administering their pay, and evaluating benefits. Someone else will address the issue of how they spend their time. Financial systems, as we have noted are focused on formulating budgets satisfactory to the Congress, and tracking the funds through execution to ensure they are not overspent. Someone else will determine if the funds are actually achieving useful results.

With the advent of public sector ERP, it may finally be someone else's turn to receive the necessary information. But the attempt to link resources with larger purposes is an old goal. Its achievement has been an evolving process, not just within the defense community but also within the larger federal community. The most important development of this type occurred with the installation of Planning, Programming, and Budgeting System (PPBS) within DoD in 1961 and within the overall Federal Government in 1965. Although it must be firmly counted as a failure in its application to the overall Federal Government, at a minimum it marks a major step towards process-oriented, results based public sector management. PPBS shared with prior budgetary paradigms the fascination with efficiency.[9] But there was a new emphasis here on aggregating the parts – personnel, facilities, equipment and supplies – into a more coherent whole: a whole that began to suggest the linkages of resources with the ultimate purposes of organization. This approach to public sector management contrasted with the traditional approach that specified the objects to be bought instead of the results to be obtained. Similar to previous attempts, there was the inevitable computation of ratios between cost and the intended purpose. However, with respect to information for performance, the important advance was the accumulation of subordinate costs into data elements for translating the constituent budget line items into a set of recognizable building blocks of organizational outputs. Separate data elements when combined with other related elements constituted a program. Accurate information was vital to successful PPBS – but its focus was elsewhere. Although it worked hard at structuring information for output and outcome oriented decisions, it often failed to address the processes that would satiate its massive demand for enterprise-wide information. PPBS were withdrawn from general use in 1970 within the Federal Government but remains in use within the DoD.

Where to Go: A Vision for Federal Government 'To-Be'

In an interview with *Government Executive* magazine, the fiscal assistant secretary at the Treasury Department expressed the opinion that Federal managers do not fully understand the value of having timely, accurate financial data.[10] This has been the opinion of Congress now for several decades. After the failure of government-wide PPBS, new doctrines of performance management began to emerge in the 1980s that echoed the PPBS focus on output orientation. Beginning in 1990, perhaps in response to the significant budget deficits of that decade, passage of several significant acts signaled new approaches to public sector performance management along with a new emphasis on the quality of management information. This series of legislation has in effect created new doctrines of government performance and financial management that move beyond the old focus on efficiency and fraud. These new doctrines, as written in the federal statutes, are fundamentally driving the current federal interest in ERP. Collectively they can constitute an end-state for the government activities as they implement ERP. The following review offers a short introduction to the key elements, statutory and otherwise, that constitute the supporting timbers of this new doctrine. All have their roots in federal statute and collectively comprise one possible vision for federal ERP.

Statutory Sources

Federal Managers Financial Integrity Act (FMFIA) of 1982: The current round of financial reform began quietly in 1982 with the passage of the FMFIA (PL 97-255). This expanded the 1950s legislation that requires each agency head to maintain accounting and internal controls systems that integrated agency accounting systems with Department of the Treasury. The FMFIA legislation directed annual reporting by agency heads on the conformance of accounting systems with Comptroller-General standards.

CFO ACT of 1990: The act created the position of Chief Financial Officer (CFO) within sixteen cabinet departments and seven other government agencies. The CFO, is nominated by the President and confirmed by the Senate. The act specified significant responsibilities for the position. CFO's are to issue audited financial statements to the Director of the Office of Management and Budget (OMB). Most significantly, the act defined one of the CFO's responsibilities to 'develop and maintain an integrated agency accounting and financial management system' that is to provide for three key objectives: (1) integration of accounting and budgeting, (2) development and reporting of cost information, and (3) enable the systematic measurement of performance.[11] This is the only reference to performance in the act, but its direction for the development of cost information with integrated accounting and budgeting systems were significant advances.

Government Performance and Results Act of 1993(GPRA): GPRA builds on the CFO Act and greatly expanded the formal doctrines of government performance.[12] It utilizes the then new emphasis on government-wide accounting directed by the CFO Act and states its purposes as seeking to mitigate: (1) waste and inefficiency undermining citizen confidence in government, (2) insufficient congressional attention to program performance and results, and, (3) 'insufficient articulation of program goals and inadequate information on program performance'.[13] The GPRA Act (PL 103-62) directed for each agency the submission of an annual performance report to the President and the Congress. Performance goals were to be set 'covering each program activity set forth in the budget of such agency'.[14] The plans require the establishment of objective and measurable program goals, performance indicators, and a process of comparing actual program results with goals. It significantly added to performance doctrines by defining within the law its definitions of output and performance.

Despite the intended development of performance plans 'for each program activity', the reality of GPRA's implementation has been much different. For example, with respect to the DoD, although clearly improving within the Bush Administration, performance reporting has been maintained at the very top levels of the department. The development of performance plans, instead of becoming an internalized process, has been largely dealt with as an external reporting requirement. For example, the DoDs FY2000 GPRA report distilled the largest government department into two performance goals: 'shaping the international environment', and 'preparing now for an uncertain future'. Neither goal was extended to lower levels.[15]

Government Management and Reform Act of 1994 (GMRA): The GMRA (PL 103-376) added a small but significant dynamic to the development of government financial information. The GPRA of the previous year had provided for annual financial statement from agencies under the CFO Act. GMRA added a significant addition to the act by requiring financial reports to be independently audited in accordance with generally accepted government accounting standards.

Federal Financial Management Improvement Act of 1996 (FFMIA): The FFMIA required federal financial management system to conform to three standards: (1) Federal Requirement, (2) Federal Accounting Standards, (3) US Standard General Ledger. The Act requires audit compliance reporting; a compliance implementation determination by the agency head, and – if an agency is in non-compliance with a standard three year plan – to bring the agency within compliance. This legislation mandated the creation of Federal Financial Improvement initiatives. The DoD began a Federal Financial Management Improvement Program (FFMIP) that published annual plans and made some progress in reducing the number of internal accounting systems used within the department. The Clinton Administration FFMIP became the Financial Management Modernization Program under Secretary Rumsfeld and was renamed the Business Management Modernization Program (BMMP) in Spring 2003.

Executive Branch Initiatives

In addition to congressional activities, there is history of executive branch initiatives that sometimes led and sometimes followed congressional action. The OMB played a dual role in the process both as an implementing organization for the new legislation and as an innovator. OMB Circular A-127, Financial Management Systems (23, July 1993), and OMB Circular A-123, Management Accountability and Control (21, June 1995) both updated 1980s circulars. Each circular concurrently built on the requirements of preceding legislation, such as the CFO Act of 1990, and then framed the issues for the next round of legislation

Other Performance Doctrine Sources

To effectively implement the CFO Act of 1990, the executive branch required a process to establish accounting standards for agency management control. The Federal Accounting Standards Advisory Board (FASAB) was established in October 1990 to evaluate and recommend accounting principles for the Federal Government. Since that time, the Board has issued several important standards as Statements of Federal Financial Accounting Standards (SFFAS). The board describes its work in the following way, 'The new reporting concepts and accounting standards that have resulted are central to effectively meeting the financial management improvement goals of the CFO Act of 1990, as amended. Also, improved financial information is necessary to support the strategic planning and performance measurement requirements of the Government Performance and Results Act (GPRA) of 1993'.[16]

In connection with the FASAB, there is a hierarchy that constitutes Generally Accepted Accounting Principles (GAAP) for the purpose of organizational auditing under the GMRA of 1994. At the highest level are the FASAB statements. When the FASAB publishes its recommendations, and they are accepted by the Department of the Treasury, the Office of Management and Budget and the Comptroller-General, they become standards constituting the highest level of authoritative guidance on Federal financial accounting. [17]

Through the approval process of OMB, the actions of the FASAB constitute a part of the executive branch institutionalization of congressionally mandated performance improvements. Of special interest here is SFFAS No. 4, 'Managerial Cost Accounting Standards and Concepts.' SFFAS No. 4 states its purpose as 'providing reliable and timely information on the full cost of federal programs, their activities, and outputs'.[18]

SFFAS No. 4 promulgates five managerial cost accounting elements: (1) requirement for cost accounting, (2) responsibility segments, (3) full cost, (4) inter-entity costs, and (5) costing methodology. These elements bring together Federal cost accounting, financial reporting, and budgeting. SFFAS No. 4 reiterates the goals of federal financial reporting to help determine the costs, efforts, and accomplishment of federal programs over time.[19] Then SFFAS No. 4 describes five purposes of using cost information in managing federal program: (1) budgeting and cost control, (2) performance measurement, (3) determining reimbursements and setting fees and prices, (4) program evaluations, and (5) making economic choice decisions.[20] The standard notes that with respect to performance measurement, 'Cost is a necessary element for performance measurement, but is not the only element'.[21] Here cost is not the end result of the process and computed as an end in itself as may have been done in the past. Instead it becomes an element of overall performance management, summarizing resource details for the larger purposes of aligning organizational resources with organizational outcomes.

Synthesizing Performance Doctrines

The emergence of public sector performance doctrine is a hopeful development when viewed from the standard of ERP. In summary, this series of legislation, along with the associated development of managerial accounting principals can be viewed to mark the formal reorientation of public sector management toward the production of specific outputs or results. There is clear direction in the doctrine for the adoption of process orientation within public sector management. This is particularly true for GPRA requirements. The General Accounting Office (GAO) confirms this in characterizing GPRA's objectives as: 'to improve the management of federal programs by shifting the focus of decision making from staffing and activity levels to the results of federal programs'.[22] Ideally, functional activities are now to be reoriented towards their final consumers and aligned with the outcomes to which they contribute.

The contributing roles of the CFO Act and the FFMIA are to improve the quality of federal financial data and combine it with the myriad of currently disconnected information that represents the outcomes of government. The combined effect is a potentially revolutionary change in public sector management. If doctrines set requirements, then this statutory foundation can be seen as having set forth new developments in government information systems and data designs that have marked the last fifteen years and three presidential administrations. This realignment of public sector performance doctrine parallels the process orientation of ERP. For this reason, this series of legislation, both individually and taken as a whole, constitutes a potentially useful vision in connection with public sector ERP change management.

NOTES

1. Office of Management and Budget. 'The President's Management Agenda – Fiscal Year 2002'. p. 28
2. OMB (2002), p. 27.
3. Quoted by Eliot Cohen in 'A Tale of Two Secretaries.' Foreign Affairs. April 2002. p. 35.
4. Cohen. P. 35
5. Department of Defense. Special briefing by Stephen Friedman, Chairman of the Board of Trustees, Columbia University and Retired Chairman of Goldman Sachs & Co., on 'Transforming Department of Defense Financial Management: A Strategy for Change.' 10, July 2001.
6. See Robert B. Denhart, Theories of Public Organization, 2nd edn. (Belmont, California, Wadsworth Publishing Company, 1993) p. 50–1, or Hal G. Rainey. Understanding and Managing Public Organizations, 3rd edn. (San Francisco, Wiley & Sons, 2003), p. 22–31.
7. US Constitution. Article 1, section 9.
8. Naval Sea Systems Command. 'Anti-Deficiency Act.'. 25, Nov. 2003. www.navsea.navy.mil/sea-01.
9. See Vincent Ostrom, The Intellectual Crisis in American Public Administration, revised edition. (University, Alabama, University of Alabama Press, 1974), p. 48–50
10. Donald Hammond, Fiscal Assistant Secretary at the Treasury Department in Matthew Weinstock, 'Erroneous Payments Cost Government $20 billion in 2001'. Government Executive.Com. 31, May, 2002. http://www.govexec.com/dailyfed/0502/053102w1.htm, Accessed 24, April 2004.
11. 31 USC Sec 902 as amended by PL 101-576.
12. See GPRA Legislative History, Senate Committee on Government Oversight (S.20). www.whitehouse.gov/omb/mgmt-gpra/gprptm.html.
13. Government Performance and Results Act of 1993. Section 2: Findings. www.whitehouse.gov/omb/mgmt-gpra/gprptm.html.

14. USC 31 Section 1115. Section entitled: 'Performance Plans'.
15. There are reports the DoD will push GPRA reporting requirement lower within the organization.
16. Staats, Elmer B. in Introduction to 'Overview of Federal Accounting Concepts and Standards (as of 30, September 1996): Reporting Relevant Financial Information'. Report No. 1. Federal Accounting Standards Advisory Board. 31, December 1996. Federal Accounting Standards Board. http://www.fasab.gov/pdffiles/con_stan.pdf
17. Department of Defense Financial Management Regulation. Volume I, Chapter 8. 'Hierarchy of Accounting Standards.' May 1998. www.defenselink.mil/comptroller/fmr/01/01_08.pdf.
18. Federal Accounting Standards Board. 'Statement of Federal Accounting Standards No. 4: Managerial Cost Accounting Standards and Concepts'. FASAB: Original Pronouncements, Version 3 (01/2004). P. 323. http://www.fasab.gov/pdffiles/vol1v3.pdf.
19. SFFAS No. 4. p. 319. FASAB: Original Pronouncements, Version 2.1 (10/2001).
20. SFFAS No. 4. p. 323 Version 2.1 (10/2001).
21. SFFAS No. 4. p. 325. Version 2.1 (10/2001).
22. Government Accountability Office. GAO/GGD-10.1.20 Guide to Assessing Agency Annual Performance Plans, April 1998 Ver. 1. p. 1.

BIBLIOGRAPHY

Cohen, Eliot (2002) 'A Tale of Two Secretaries.' Foreign Affairs. April.
Denhart, Robert B. (1993), Theories of Public Organization, 2nd edn. Belmont, California, Wadsworth Publishing Company,
Federal Accounting Standards Board, 'Statement of Federal Accounting Standards No. 4: Managerial Cost Accounting Standards and Concepts.' FASAB: Original Pronouncements, Version 3 (01/2004). P. 323. http://www.fasab.gov/pdffiles/vol1v3.pdf
Hammond, Donald (2002), Fiscal Assistant Secretary at the Treasury Department quoted in Matthew Weinstock, 'Erroneous Payments Cost Government $20 billion in 2001'. Government Executive.Com. 31 May, www.govexec.com/dailyfed/0502/053102w1.htm. Accessed 24 April, 2004.
Naval Sea Systems Command (2003), 'Anti-Deficiency Act', 25 Nov. www.navsea.navy.mil/sea-01.
Office of Management and Budget (2002) The President's Management Agenda – Fiscal Year 2002.
Ostrom, Vincent (1974), The Intellectual Crisis in American Public Administration, revised edition. University, Alabama, University of Alabama Press.
Rainey, Hal G. (2003), Understanding and Managing Public Organizations, 3rd edn. San Francisco, Wiley & Sons.
Staats, Elmer B. (1996), in Introduction to 'Overview of Federal Accounting Concepts and Standards (as of 30, September 1996): Reporting Relevant Financial Information'. Report No. 1. Federal Accounting Standards Advisory Board. 31 December. Federal Accounting Standards Board. http://www.fasab.gov/pdffiles/con_stan.pdf
US Department of Defense (1998), 'Hierarchy of Accounting Standards'. Financial Management Regulation. Volume I, Chapter 8, May, www.defenselink.mil/comptroller/fmr/01/01_08.pdf
US Department of Defense (2001), 'Transforming Department of Defense Financial Management: A Strategy for Change'. Special briefing by Stephen Friedman.

PART II

CONSULTING VIEW

5. Challenges of Implementing Enterprise Resource Planning Applications within the Department of Defense

Micheline Lopez-Estrada

INTRODUCTION

In July 2001 the Secretary of Defense issued a mandate to begin business transformation and announced business transformation as one of the Department's top ten priorities. As a result the Department of Defense (DoD) awarded a contract for the financial management enterprise architecture initiative, now called the Business Enterprise Architecture (BEA). This ambitious undertaking designed to consolidate and standardize all of DOD's financial reporting systems delivered an initial architecture (BEA 1.0) on April 2003, one year after the contract was awarded. The original intent of this initiative was focused on financial processes only, however, in the process of designing the initial architecture it became evident that this was not an effective way to drive business process reengineering from an enterprise perspective. There was not a clean cut financial business process perspective, hence an end-to-end view of business processes was selected. The initiative was then 'redirected' to include all business processes in six major business areas known as 'Domains'. These domains are: accounting and finance (ACC & FIN), acquisition (ACQ), human resource management (HRM), installations and environment (I&E), logistics (LOG) and strategic planning and budgeting (SPB).

The version 2.0 of the Department-wide Business Enterprise Architecture was delivered on February 2004 and is pending government approval. The BEA objective is:

To serve as the blueprint that enables streamlined processes and integrated systems to transform the way the Department conducts its business. The Business Enterprise Architecture is designed to ensure compliance with appropriate laws, regulations, policies, and standards, as well as to provide additional detail to govern DoD business operations. It embodies the DoD's vision of where it wants to be, by documenting the requirements of the future business environment. Fundamental similarities in core DoD business management functions across the Services and

Defense Agencies make Business Enterprise Architecture development critical. Therefore, business process and systems integration will enable the Department to re-direct millions of dollars in support of national security through increased efficiencies, elimination of redundant activities and systems, and improved decision-making capabilities.[1]

Prior to the DoD mandate many Federal agencies and DoD components were realizing and recognizing that they must manage their work processes to look across the entire agency in a horizontal view. This is in addition to the traditional functional or vertical view. Much of this realization came as a result of other government initiatives such as the e-Government initiative. This realization started an explosion of business process re-engineering initiatives and enterprise architecture definition efforts within the department agencies. Many organizations within the DoD started these efforts prior to the Secretary of Defense mandate and much earlier than the DoD's initial delivery of the Department-wide Business Enterprise Architecture. These non-integrated efforts have already fielded several ERP systems across DoD components and many more are under development. This is creating an interesting management and technical challenge for DoD Business Management Modernization Program (BMMP) efforts and for the DoD Components ERP initiatives.

As in commercial ERP implementations, the Government ERP implementations face many challenges during the life cycle of their efforts. Many of these challenges are common between the private and the public sector; however there is some uniqueness in each one of the challenges in the public sector implementations.

Objective

This chapter presents challenges that the DoD Components and Federal agencies confront when implementing an ERP initiative. Some of these challenges are common within ERP implementations in the private and public sector. Challenges unique within the public sector are also discussed. Specifically, challenges addressed in this chapter are:

1. Lack of long-term architecture and operational vision;
2. Lack of understanding of current system landscape and portfolio management processes;
3. Mandated system interfaces;
4. Too much scope – the 'big-bang' approach;
5. The government budgeting process;
6. Team expertise – scarcity of resources and personnel skill sets;

7. Leadership commitment and support;
8. The decentralization within an organization;
9. Lack of system integrator understanding of government business processes;
10. The 'blind leading the blind' syndrome;
11. Immature mandated compliancy requirements; and
12. Lack of a data management strategy.

THE CHALLENGES

Lack of Long-Term Architecture and End-State Operational Vision

Defining your enterprise business process architecture is critical when implementing an ERP solution. The architecture will identify and define business processes by developing an understanding of the scope of the initiative. This information not only helps in identifying the scope of the effort, but also will help with the selection of the software application, by highlighting potential functional gaps. Some understanding of the 'as-is' business process is necessary in order to support the re-engineering effort during the blueprinting-requirement definition phase. Not knowing or understanding how processes are currently conducted in the organization can lead to long discussions, which drive schedule slips and cost increases. Understanding where the organization is from a business process perspective will help to determine where the organization wants to be at the end of the implementation. Therefore, it is important to define the end-state from an operational vision perspective. The final business process architecture should be based on leading business practices. These leading business practices represent a new set of business processes, business rules, policies and procedures that define how the organization will perform its business.

Getting agreement on the 'to-be' processes and the business rules governing those processes is essential for success. Many Government agencies have started the implementation of ERP applications as replacements of legacy systems versus traditional enterprise re-engineering events. As such, many efforts have been started without the benefit of a clear understanding of the organizational business architecture. After the painful realization of the integrated nature of modern ERP software, many teams saw the need for a better understanding of how different business processes would fit within the end-state enterprise business process architecture. In many cases the definition of the architecture was initiated after the organization had already deployed an ERP implementation and realized that the organization did not achieve the envisioned benefits. This 'after-the-fact' effort leads to many changes in the current implementation, thereby creating a chaotic and unstable environment for the organization. This eventually results in losing customer satisfaction and increased maintenance costs due to the number of interfaces that need to be maintained in order to achieve end-to-end business processes. In addition, many of the DoD ERP efforts started prior to the DoD's initial delivery of the Department-wide Business Enterprise Architecture; thereby leaving the Department Components to freely make enterprise level decisions at the Component level. This early lack of direction impacted both the DoD BEA effort and the individual DoD Component ERP efforts by hampering the desired DoD-wide integrated business architecture goals. It will be a challenge to achieve those goals if applications are being developed without an understanding of the end vision and without mature requirements.

Understanding the 'end-state' operational vision from the inception of the program is a critical factor in determining how large the implementation will be, and what is the best implementation and deployment approach to take for the organization. The enterprise business process architecture will facilitate the definition of the operational vision and facilitates the development of an achievable implementation roadmap; thereby avoiding the classic mistake of trying to implement in a 'big-bang' manner. Investing early on the definition of a business process architecture for the organization will support management of the legacy systems portfolio, support cross-domain process integration and facilitate identification and understanding of interfaces.

Many private sector implementations also face this challenge, however it is more difficult in the private sector to spend millions of dollars on stovepipe solutions than in the public sector. The private sector has a more effective management structure for controlling business systems investments.

Lack of Understanding of Current System Landscape and a Portfolio Management Process

Many organizations start their enterprise resources planning (ERP) efforts without expending the time in understanding the processes they want to re-engineer, and without an understanding of their current system landscape. Understanding the current system landscape, and getting the necessary expertise to support the required legacy system documentation in the Business Process Re-engineering (BPR) effort will improve the chances for success. The lack of understanding on these critical BPR tenets, make the BPR effort a very difficult task. Many Government implementations start at the domain levels instead of at the enterprise level, because the organization approaches the ERP implementation from a functional or vertical perspective instead of a horizontal, end-to-end business process view. For example, a department can be working on a human resource implementation, or in a financial management implementation and/or a logistics implementation. This approach usually brings requirement control challenges to the implementation; not only for the fragmented approach taken, but also from a lack of understanding of the legacy systems executing these vertical processes. Many systems have been developed to deal with one area, for example, account payable, time and attendance, training, and maintenance. These systems have to interface to other systems to complete with the organizational end-to-end business process loop. All these systems were developed as customized systems to fulfill a mission; none of them were developed with an enterprise architecture view in mind. In many cases multiple systems have been developed to fill gaps identified in other systems, thus creating a complex spaghetti architecture of 'system of systems', which is very difficult to manage. Adding to these risks is also the lack of a mature portfolio management process within Government organizations which facilitates the migration of the legacy systems in a more organized fashion. This lack of understanding usually drives an increase in business requirements, which in turn increases the implementation costs, and ultimately creates schedule slips.

The uniqueness of this public sector challenge is evident when we look at the number of 'mandated systems' that an organization has to interface with. This challenge is independent of the fact that the functions could be performed within their local ERP application, because federal law mandates interfacing. Hence, there no cost savings. Most of these systems are not owned by the organization implementing the ERP application, which makes the negotiation process on what to interface to, and which system needs to be added to a system landscape, more interesting than in the private sector. These mandated interfaces complicate the system landscape in which ERP applications will be operating.

Mandated System Interfaces

There are many initiatives and established programs that impact any ERP implementation within Government agencies. Organizations are required to interface to external and DoD mandated systems. Internal systems not replaced by ERP software and external entities such as vendors or customers, minimize in some cases the utilization of the integrated processes nature that an ERP product offers. Most of these legacy programs and initiatives were not developed with an enterprise architecture vision in mind, creating a fragmented enterprise. To comply with these mandated systems, ERP initiatives have to develop complex interfaces to be able to accomplish end-to-end business processes. This forced approach minimizes the utilization of an 'out of the box solution' which complicates the implementation with customized development.

Interfaces are the 'long pole' in most ERP implementations; not only because of the complexity of the required interfaces, but also due to the programmatic complexity when dealing with development that has to occur across departments and/or other Government organizations. The amount of coordination required to accomplish the development of an interface is tremendous. Once the interfaces requirements have been identified, the second challenge is identifying appropriate stakeholders and developing a mutually acceptable interface memorandum of agreement, which usually takes some time to put in place. The average development cost of a highly complex system interface can range between US$500K–1M, and there are Government ERP initiatives that have identified and/or developed over 50 critical systems interfaces. The cost burden on these implementations from this one component alone can be enormous. There is no effective DoD process in place that allows the services to share and reuse interface objects. This leads to the duplication of development and eventual high costs.

With many Government ERP initiatives being developed in parallel and without a mature enterprise architecture in place, it is inevitable that there are redundant interface development efforts. This custom development cycle usually increases the original scope of the implementation because most of these new requirements are not discovered until after the blueprinting phase is completed. In addition, the real complexity of those systems interfaces is not realized until the realization phase, when the teams start the development of the customized interface objects. This effort usually adds many more new requirements to the original scope.

The uniqueness in this challenge in the public sector is better described by the following statement from a US General Accounting Office (GAO) report to Congress.

> DoD does not have a central repository or systematic process for identifying all of the department's systems. Without an accurate inventory of existing systems and with uncertainty as to whether all business system funding is reflected in the IT budget, it is not surprising that DOD has yet to establish an effective management oversight structure and processes to control its ongoing and planned business systems investments.[2]

Too Much Scope – The 'Big-Bang' Approach

Many Government ERP implementations try to implement too much functionality, or scope at once. Hence, it becomes almost impossible to achieve success within the mandates of the defined program schedule, which in turn creates a very long stabilization process before the project team can declare implementation success. In most cases, this is due to a lack of understanding of the current business processes, and a lack of vision concerning the organizational 'end-state view' of the implementation. This all translates into a lack of the long-term architecture design and the end-state operational vision. As the implementation teams discover new gaps and new legacy systems, the associated new requirements keep piling onto the implementation project plan, thereby creating a 'super build' which needs to be accommodated in the original program schedule. The lack of an early implementation roadmap and end vision creates just another challenge for the implementation to overcome. Having an implementation roadmap can facilitate the identification of incremental or spiral development builds that will help to mitigate the risks of too much scope for the implementation. For most Government implementations the Return On Investment (ROI) on an ERP implementation comes from the retirement of legacy systems. The more legacy systems an organization can retire, the more maintenance costs it saves. Therefore, managing the scope of the implementation is a very challenging effort that the program manager has to prioritize in order to achieve both an achievable scope and an acceptable ROI.

The Government Budgeting Process

The Government budgeting process is a very long and complicated process and begins well over a year in advance of the beginning of the fiscal year. The cycle starts with the development of budget requests by the Government agencies. In addition to this process, the agencies also have to deal with 'color of money' (different appropriations) issues. Since the implementation methodology of an ERP implementation consists of different phases; the true costs are only known during the second phase (the blueprinting-requirement gathering phase). Only at this stage does the organization really understand the scope of the project and when they really can estimate the total cost of the implementation. In the Government, the organization trying to implement an ERP program has to 'guess' how much the implementation is going to cost in advance of knowing their final scope. This process leads to a guessing approach which usually tends to underestimate the implementation requirements in order to get the funds necessary to start the implementation. Usually one of the challenges is that the cost estimate is done in-house, with resources that are used to estimating traditional software development efforts, and does not understand the true nature of an ERP implementation. As the implementation of the ERP initiative is probably going to be competed within industry, no participation is permitted from contractors that may be potential bidders. This process offers big challenges to the program managers and makes it very difficult to estimate an unknown requirement.

As the Government deals with different appropriations or 'colors of money', and expiration dates for funds, another challenge arises. If for any reason the implementation schedule slips, and the program now does not have the correct color of money or funds, time has expired and the implementation is stalled. If the program is under-spending their funds, then the program runs the risk of losing the funding. As there is no reward program in place for saving or holding funds, it becomes a challenge to the creativeness and imagination of the program manager to overcome the burdens imposed by the government budget and financial processes. As in the private sector:

> from a political standpoint, the persistent budget deficit that has become a permanent feature of federal public finance is unpopular, leading to calls for reductions in overall spending independent of the merits of individual programs. As in private finance, possible areas of public spending must be weighed against one another in light of the opportunity cost of raising resources to pay for the program.[3]

The public sector has to deal with more constraints because once an agency gets the funding for the implementation there is less flexibility to modify the execution of those funds regardless if it is the right thing to do.

Team Expertise – Scarcity of Resources and Personnel Skill Sets

In most ERP implementations the teams are composed of system integrator personnel and team members from within the organization that is implementing the application. The roles of each team member are identified, and the team is established during the project preparation phase of an ERP implementation. As the implementation progresses through the life-cycle phases the teams get populated with more resources. Mostly, the Government needs to identify personnel to fill two major roles: (a) organization functional expertise, which depends on the business processes being re-engineered, and (b) program management expertise to manage the effort. In most cases the organization will have to draw resources from across the organization departments in order to support an ERP implementation. This requires corporation commitment and support.

One of the challenges an organization encounters during this process is getting the right people with the right skills to support the implementation. In most cases the department responsible for the implementation requests the human resources from other departments and/or programs within the organization. There is a tendency to provide resources that 'can be spared' or resources the organization does not want to manage anymore. This presents a big challenge during the implementation because the people 'driving' the business process change, frequently lack the required expertise and experience from the organizational business process perspective. In the area of program management the Government has the responsibility of providing the management, monitoring, and oversight role for the ERP implementation contract. Finding the right people that not only have functional expertise but also have program management expertise represents a challenge during an implementation. This creates an environment where program management tenets may not be followed, leading to cost and schedule increases.

These challenges are not different from a private sector implementation. However, what is different from a Government perspective is the monumental effort required to remove a resource from a project when it is not performing. This also points to the fact that there is the lack of a reward system that ties employee performance to the organizational strategic goals. The Government has been working on various initiatives that address issues concerning the management and rewards of human capital. The US Office of Personnel Management (OPM) has several initiatives underway 'to improve Federal recruitment, hiring, and retention and to focus on meaningful performance distinctions as the key drivers for human resources and reward decisions. Those reform efforts have surfaced recurring themes concerning the constraints and contradictions the pay system imposes'. The OPM agency has identified how Government employees get rewarded as one of the failing areas of the agency. The agency stated, 'It has minimal ability to encourage and reward achievement and results. Over 75 percent of the increase in Federal pay bears no relationship to individual achievement or competence'.[4] Building a team to implement an ERP under this environment is a challenging task and requires complete leadership commitment and support to provide the 'best talent' for the implementation and to identify the ERP initiative as one of the organizational strategic goals.

Leadership Commitment and Support

To have a successful implementation, support is required from the top of the organization from the inception of the implementation initiative. Time, dedication and active participation are required in order to achieve standardization across the organization. To maximize exploitation of the capabilities an ERP package offers, process re-engineering activities need to be conducted and adoption of best business practices need to be considered. To make this change management effort successful, executive support is essential. Most important is the establishment of an executive process council to provide oversight and approval of proposed business processes changes and business rules adoption. The executive body will facilitate the change management effort within the organization and across organizations. In large Government organizations getting support from all the required leaders can be a challenge. The process of determining process owners and ownership can be quite overwhelming. However, 'there is a direct correlation between active sponsorship and success in any major organizational change'.[5] Many ERP projects go underway without a clear definition and identification of an Executive Process Board. Having an Executive Process Board from the program inception will allow the organization to maximize the standardization across the organization, develop and maintain enterprise architecture and related business process and data standards, and maximize their return on investment. In Government organizations, top executive support is critical, because in some cases adoption of best business practices and standards will require statute, regulatory, and/or policy changes. This overarching set of requirements present an extraordinary challenge when implementing an ERP application within the Government, due to the amount of organizations and people that need to be involved and convinced in order to modify or adjust the overarching requirement. Without top executive support this challenge will become impossible to overcome; jeopardizing business process re-engineering efforts and adopting inefficient business processes as 'to be' solutions. Therefore, executive process owners (team leads) need to build coalitions with internal and external stakeholders in order to facilitate the mitigation strategies on these risks. Executive process owners need to get an early understanding of the implementation business process requirements and end operational architecture vision in order to serve as a change management agent for the effort.

The Decentralization Within an Organization and Across Organizations

In order to successfully implement an ERP application, each organization and/or department within the agency must be willing to make compromises and agree to business process standardization, data standards, and standard operating procedures for the good of the entire organization. Management commitment in this area is vital for the Agency to realize the optimal benefits from the investment in this effort. The lack of early recognition of the existing culture, which usually can be described as highly decentralized and autonomous in most of the federal agencies and DoD components, drive schedule slips and cost increases. This decentralization of investments and enterprise level management decisions create a very challenging environment for an ERP application implementation from an issue resolution process perspective. It will take a paramount amount of work to get an enterprise decision from Government organizations. There are many 'interested' parties who must be consulted and each one of them has a unique agenda. This is reflected in reality for there are many Government agencies with multiple ERP implementations, implementing applications in a vertical approach fashion (a financial management, a human resources management effort). The lack of a centralized overarching organization responsible for managing the enterprise business integration within each of the DoD Components usually leads to disintegrated systems. This problem occurs within an organization and across organizations in the Government. The DoD establishment of the DoD BMMP office is a potential solution to this challenge; once they get their business architecture mature enough to be able to guide the other initiatives.

Lack of System Integrator Understanding of Government Business Processes

Most of the system integrators responsible for an ERP implementation have expertise on ERP applications and implementation methodologies, and sometimes some experience with Government business processes. That is the reason why in an ERP implementation, the implementation teams consist of systems integrator members and members from within the organization implementing the application. If the Government does not identify its best talent to participate during the implementation, then it is up to the systems integrator to try to figure out the best approach for re-engineering and implementing a business process. Many times this approach does not work in the best interest of the Government. Government business processes are complex and convoluted due to fact that they have evolved and have been fragmented over the last 50 years. Many systems have been developed to deal with one area; for example, accounts payable, time and attendance, etc. All these systems were developed as customized systems to fulfill a mission; none were developed with an enterprise view in mind. In many cases multiple systems have been developed to fill gaps identified in other systems thereby creating a convoluted architecture (a system of systems), which is very difficult to manage. Most integrators start into this effort without really understanding the current Government system landscape and the systems applications within that landscape. After the blueprinting requirements gathering phase, the realization of the complexities of the interfaces is identified, and reality hits the systems integrator. In order to eliminate a system and/or interface to a system, an understanding of that system is essential. In many instances the Government organization implementing the ERP does not own those required systems. As a result, neither side really has the expertise necessary to move forward; commencing a cycle of discovery that is late in the process. As a result, in many Government implementations the management of these gaps becomes a challenge, which ultimately plays a major role on schedule and cost increases. It is essential that open communication between the systems integrator and the Government team is fostered from the inception of the program. Lacking mitigation plans for these risk areas is one of the major mistakes both the Government and system integrators consistently make. A clear understanding on expertise provided by both teams has to be clearly identified at the beginning of the project in order to contract for any shortfall of expertise.

Public sector business processes and legacy systems are complex and many of them have to comply with policies, regulations and laws. For this and other reasons, it takes specific expertise to be able to determine the best way to take advantage of leading best practices offered by ERP applications.

The 'Blind Leading the Blind' Syndrome

The Government understands that it does not have experience in managing ERP implementations; therefore, they usually contract out to compensate for this shortfall. Hence, many companies have identified themselves as 'trusted agents' to support the Government in this endeavor. The support provided by these companies is in the areas of program management, business re-engineering, portfolio management, and architecture development and management. In many instances, the Government utilizes the companies that they already have on their 'payroll' (under contract), which does not necessarily translate into the necessary expertise for this type of effort. In other instances the Government extends the role of a company, which was contracted for a particular area of expertise, to other roles where they lack expertise. Again, the Government tends to continue drawing support from existing contract resources and one of the reasons for this approach maybe is due to the complex contracting process within the Government. This cycle leads to what is called the 'blind leading the blind' syndrome, which usually leads to schedule slips and cost increases.

A similar syndrome also occurs at the oversight level of the Government. Organizations such as the DoD BMMP organization, which has been identified as the oversight organization to manage these efforts, does not have a mature BEA developed; yet they are trying to lead the DoD Components on their enterprise business initiatives. This cycle of trying to comply with immature requirements leads to the 'blind leading the blind' syndrome once again. There are many meetings where much gets discussed but the realities of the impact on the decisions being made are hard to discover because the overarching requirements are not fully defined. It will be very difficult for both the DoD Components and the BMMP initiative to achieve the desired level of business integration if this pattern continues.

Immature Mandated Compliance Requirements

To succeed, enterprise architecture initiatives will require meeting overarching attributes, rules and processes not only for technical architectures but also for business architectures. These compliancy requirements must be mature enough for sub-enterprise architectures to follow and 'comply' to. The DoD has been in the process of developing a department-wide architecture since 2001. However, after three years of this initiative the Department is still lacking a mature governance model, communication and guidelines, standards, training, and architecture requirements for the Components to successfully comply. In order for the Components to make a significant contribution to the DoD architecture business goals, an environment needs to be created in which this can be achieved. The factors that make an enterprise architecture effort successful are outlined in the Gartner paper (2002), 'Seven Architecture Management Best Practices'.

> The way that enterprise architecture is managed is key to its success. Excellent technical work that is not aligned with business objectives, or which is ignored by projects, will be wasted. The seven steps described here – consistent architecture processes and a process to assess exceptions; the right governance model; review architecture standards and guidelines regularly; communicate architecture goals; communicate processes, standards and guidelines widely; enterprise architecture contributing to business planning, and create an environment in which enterprise architecture can make a significant contribution to business goals.[6]

The DoD BMMP initiative needs to get ahead of the DoD Components that are implementing ERP projects in order for the Department to achieve the desired business integration goals without spending too much money on current implementations that may or may not contribute to the overall goals.

Lack of a Data Management Strategy

> Due to the integrated nature of SAP itself, as well as the inter-relationships of master data and the enterprise business processes, it is critical that an organization recognize this and put in place an approach, as well as a team structure, to ensure integration of the overall enterprise design with the master data objects.[7]

This statement is true and applicable to any ERP application implementation. Data management is a critical factor to have a successful ERP implementation. Government organizations have an enormous amount of data distributed across multiple legacy systems. In many Government implementations data management is not addressed from an enterprise data model perspective but instead the focus is on data exchange and required translation layers from an interface perspective. This approach usually focuses on interfacing systems instead of focusing on integrating systems with an underlying data management strategy to achieve data standardization across the enterprise landscape. As a result, this effort is usually one of the 'last efforts' to be addressed from an enterprise perspective. Data standards are critical for ERP implementation to succeed in an integrated environment.

RECOMMENDATIONS

Define and Document Your Enterprise Business Architecture

- Understand your current system landscape and business processes in order to maximize your re-engineering/process improvements efforts. Enterprise applications invite multiple functional scope approaches (finance, procurement, supply chain management, project management) to optimize their use. Limiting scope to a single or a few functions causes issues by 'disintegrating' the product resulting in excessive interfaces to legacy systems. Functional and vertical views also limit the opportunity to 'retire' legacy systems. Alternatively, end-to-end views result in better integration and solution utilization. The key is to model your Business Process Architecture in order to define your implementation and deployment roadmap in terms of scope to realize transformational results, economics related to product utilization, and benefits while considering change management impacts.
- Model your 'as-is', at least to understand your organization business process groups. This readily allows identification of your process improvement areas and ROI.
- The Business Process Architecture will help you.
- Foster the communication and coordination required to support your organizational business transformation.
- Support management of IT portfolios.
- Support Cross-Enterprise Integration.
- Think from an Enterprise view from the beginning and define the Enterprise early and clearly.
- Identify and understand your interfaces early.

Executive Leadership Support

- Top management sponsorship from the inception of the program is critical to ensure that the vision and architecture are in concert with the corporate business strategic goals. A Process Owners Executive Council is essential to implement the required organization changes in order to maximize the implementation return on investment.

Establish Key Metrics and Use Them

- Metrics and targets for the expected results are key to driving business process re-engineering, improving performance, tracking results, and communicating benefits throughout the program implementation. Their value increases throughout the program and are indispensable to keep the program and team focused. Tie measures to higher level balanced scorecards and strategies.
- A comprehensive and detailed schedule is critical to manage the program. Includes time for all elements especially during the testing phase. Allocate time for unit test, stress test, integration (including live data conversion) testing and security test.

Integration and Standardization

- Adopting an enterprise standardization strategy around the project will deliver significant economies of scale and maximizes the ROI of your implementation. Defining standardized global business processes, organizational and master data objects will facilitate architecture integration across the enterprise. A balance between central governance and local preference in all aspects of the implementation is essential to achieve optimization and integration. Defining a master data model is a critical factor to achieve master data integration and eliminate data reconciliation processes.

Select Your Team

- Significant in-house participation is required throughout the program life cycle. Top-level advocacy is needed to make this happen.
- Use the systems integrator team to provide some guidance and expertise where needed but make sure you 'own' the business process re-engineering decisions and understand the consequences of those decisions.

- Get the enterprise solution vendor directly involved with the program. Make them a key stakeholder and hold them accountable for the quality of their product.
- Obtain independent advice from people with hands-on experience with ERP in the DoD domain. Use this team throughout the program. This will help to educate the internal team, keep the systems integrator focused, provide 'trusted agent' advice, and help with the overall strategic planning and program execution.
- Business Process Leads and other Technical Leads must have functional expertise and good project management skills. They must be able to plan and manage resources, identify and mitigate risks and issues, deliver products and complete tasks on schedule, and stick with the overall program plan.
- Ensuring retention of the highly talented staff will be a key on allowing your organization to support a strategy of using in-house expertise to deliver, and later maintain the program with minimum systems integrator personnel.

Manage your Scope and Deployment

- Develop an implementation roadmap at the inception of the program.
- Phasing in your deployment will minimize disruptions and will give you the opportunity to improve your implementation before a large number of users come on-line. Post go-live complications and work required to stabilize the solution and build user confidence and competency in the new business process are always underestimated. Assume worst case and staff accordingly until the post go-live situation is truly understood. Do not expand the solution in scope or user base until an acceptable level of utility, user adoption, and stability is achieved.

Change Management Does Not End at the Go-Live Mark

- The number one barrier to successfully implementing an enterprise resource planning system is the resistance to change from the organization. Often the users are unfamiliar with the new system and will doubt its necessity. They are reluctant to learn new ways of doing business. Not having a change management program during implementation can be a big mistake since it is the least expensive part of the project, yet it one of the most important. The more money, time and effort put into a change management program, the greater the end results of the system as a whole.[1]

- Change management does not end with the go-live milestone a major effort is required during the go-live event and during the stabilization phase.

Define your Data Management Strategy Early[8]

- Identify and integrate data team members with the business process teams. The goal of these data team members is to drive integration across process teams by the nature of standardizing the master data.
- Establish highest level of data commonality to drive the greatest level of integration and standardization.
- Detailed data definitions must account for both ERP applications and non-ERP applications data.
- Include current data owners and key data users in the data definition. Account for both ERP application and legacy systems application data.
- Clearly define policies, guidelines, roles and responsibilities.
- Get buy-in and sign-off on the proposed data policies, guidelines and organization requirements.
- Identify your data conversion requirements early.
- Data cleansing is critical for success. Start early in the process and involve data owners in the process.

Interfaces Development Management

- Identify the expertise required from Legacy systems during the blueprinting phase.
- Identify funding to pay for the support of external agencies during the development of the interfaces.
- Minimize (to the greatest extent possible) the number of interfaces.
- A Memorandum of Agreement (MOA) is required to establish a business agreement whenever there are dependent milestones that drive each other's activities. The MOA should include the following information:
- Scope of effort covered by the MOA.
- Identify roles and responsibilities.
- Schedule, particularly milestones that mark the boundaries of 'hand-over' items.
- Clearly identify and document all expected deliverables.
- Identify areas of risk.
- Identify costs (who is responsible for the cost of the interface development or cost sharing agreements).

- Identify resources (who is responsible for any software, hardware, consultants, etc.).
- Clarify/document assumptions.
- Garner signatures on milestone deliverables.
- Describe interface and data requirements.
- Identify Middleware tools.

CONCLUSION

ERP application implementations are complex and costly regardless of whether they are being implemented in the private or public sector. They bring a number of challenges that an organization has to overcome in order to have a successful implementation. Many of these challenges are the same for both sectors. However, the public sector brings their own uniqueness to these common challenges, making their implementation process more complex.

ERP applications are enabling technologies and implementing these applications requires major organizational changes. The reason to take on an ERP implementation in private industries is to improve financial performance by increasing the company's productive capacity. This is achieved not only by eliminating non-value-adding processes but also by reducing human capital. On the other hand, many of the Government ERP implementations are seen as a means of cutting costs by reducing the number of legacy systems and not necessary by reducing human capital. Often this outlook at the end does not deliver to the Government the expected improvements leaving the organization with sub-optimized processes, multiples interfaces and manual interventions.[1]

The DoD Business Enterprise Architecture goal is to serve as a blueprint for the DoD Components by providing them business processes, business rules, standards and guidance for the Components to use as a framework on their BPR efforts. Until this point, the DoD Components have been ahead of DoD on their ERP efforts, deploying efforts that may not result in enterprise solutions that will contribute toward the end-state vision of the DoD BEA.

NOTES

1. www.dod.mil/comptroller/bmmp. Architecture Overview Page.
2. United States General Accounting Office Report to Congress Requesters GAP-04-615, May 2004. DOD Business Systems Modernization. Billions Continue to Be Invested with Inadequate Management Oversight and Accountability.
3. Chapter 17, The Governing Budgeting Process, http://garnet.acns.fsu.edu/~holcombe/chapter17.doc.
4. US Office Personnel Management, White Paper, a Fresh Start for Federal Pay: The Case for Modernization. April 2002.
5. E-Business and ERP Transforming the Enterprise, PriceWaterhouseCoopers. 2000.
6. Gartner, White Paper, Seven Architecture Management Best Practices, COM-18-9663 G.

James; 31 December 2002
7. Data Design and Management White Paper, Deloitte Consulting. 2001.
8. Most recommendations are from and/or adapted from the Data Design and Management White Paper, Deloitte Consulting. 2001.

BIBLIOGRAPHY

Data Design and Management White Paper, Deloitte Consulting. 2001.

DoD ERP Implementation Lesson Learned White Paper, Enterprise Resource Performance Inc (ERPi), R. Volker and M. Lopez-Estrada. 2004.

E-Business and ERP, Transforming the Enterprise, G. Norris, J.R. Hurley, K.M. Hartley, J.R. Dunleavy, and J.D. Balls; John Wiley and Sons, Inc. 2000 by PriceWaterhouseCoopers.

Gartner, White Paper, Seven Architecture Management Best Practices, COM-18-9663, G. James; 31 December 2002.

Http://garnet.acns.fsu.edu/~holcombe/chapter17.doc. Chapter 17, The Governing Budgeting Process.

Http://www.change-management.org/articles.htm. Change Management Resource Library.

United States General Accounting Office Report to Congress Requesters – GAP-04-615, DOD Business Systems Modernization. Billions Continue to Be Invested with Inadequate Management Oversight and Accountability, May 2004.

US Office Personnel Management, White Paper, A Fresh Start for Federal Pay: The Case for Modernization. April 2002.

www.dod.mil/comptroller/bmmp. Architecture Overview Page.

6. Business Process Change Management for ERP and other Public Sector Projects

Matthias Kirchmer

CHANGE MANAGEMENT – WHAT IT REALLY IS

All changes in an organization, in the private as well as in the public sector, require the according modifications or creations of business processes.[1] The goal of change management is to ensure that the necessary changes of a business process fulfill the following conditions:[2]

- Necessary actions are initiated with an acceptable delay after the change has happened.
- Necessary actions are executed in a fast and effective way.
- All reactions and actions are initiated and executed in a controlled manner.

An effective management of the permanent change becomes a key success-factor for an organization. It is of fundamental importance that the people involved in changing processes are able to understand and accept those changes and make them finally happen. Therefore the most appropriate definition of change management is:[3]

- Information.
- Communication.
- Training.

People have to be informed about the changes. Then their feedback is required. An intense communication starts. And finally people have to be trained to be successful in the new business process environment. Figure 6.1 shows this basic definition of change management.

Change management activities are always related to specific processes. The business processes involved in change management activities can be identified by using process reference models[4], which also exist for the defense sector.

The content of the relevant information, communication, and training concerning specific business processes can be structured using the ARIS Architecture.[5] The major questions that have to be addressed in change management activities can be directly deducted from ARIS as shown in Figure 6.2:

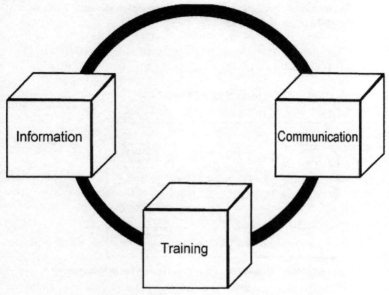

Figure 6.1: Change Management – The Activities

- Who (people, departments, different enterprises...) is involved in the change (Organization view)?
- What are the new or modified activities (function view)?
- What new or modified information is needed or produced (data view)?
- Which new or modified deliverables are expected (deliverable view)?
- How do the changes fit together and how do they influence the process logic (control view)?

PREPARING INFORMATION, COMMUNICATION, AND TRAINING

Starting point of all change management activities are information and communication. Both have to be adapted to the cultural environment of the enterprise. Here some general guidelines:[6]

- Segment the audience: different groups of people have to be addressed differently.
- Use multiple channels: people have personal preference from where they like to get their news.

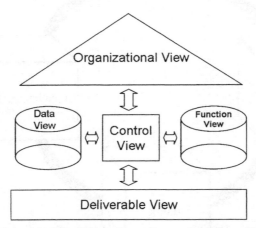

Figure 6.2: ARIS – Business Process Framework for Change Management

- Use multiple voices: switch between various 'messengers' who may each address people in another style which facilitates a high level of acceptance.
- Be clear: set clear expectations to avoid later disappointments.
- Honesty is the only policy: sooner or later people will find out the truth anyway.
- Use emotions, not just logic: you are dealing with human beings.
- Encourage: change is always difficult; nevertheless people have to feel good to be successful.
- Make the message tangible: tell people what will change definitely for them and their work environment.
- Listen, listen, and listen: your people may know more about their processes than you.

The basis for applying all these guidelines is the segmentation of the audience. Once you know exactly whom you address, you can optimize your information and communication procedures. Basic questions to guide the segmentation of an audience are the following:

- Who is in the segment?
- How will people be affected?

- What reaction will they have to it?
- What behaviors will we need from them?
- How can we stimulate these behaviors?
- When shall we inform/communicate?
- What medium should we use for each message?
- Who should communicate the message?

Challenges for successful change management activities result from disbelief, false familiarity, fear, the 'rumor mill', incomprehensibility, abstraction, complexity, and the use of clichés. Information and communication prepare the way for training activities. Those have also to be organized in a business process oriented way and address the relevant changes of today's processes. Business process oriented training can be divided up into four major phases:[7]

- Basic training – business.
- Basic training – enabler.
- Process training.
- Kick-off training.

In the basic business training the changing business background is explained. This allows people to understand the motivation for the change and ensures that they have the required general business know how. The basic 'enabler' training is an introduction into new technologies or other enablers to be used in the changed processes. This training phase includes topics like the handling of application software products or the use of new process performance tools. The core-training phase is the process training. These training activities explain how to use the process enablers in the changed business environment. It basically trains all aspects concerning the execution of the new business processes. Shortly before executing the planned change a kick-off training is recommended. It ensures that people recall the key aspects of the change and know what to do in case of problems. The structure of the business process oriented training is shown in Figure 6.3.

METHODS AND TOOLS FOR THE REALIZATION

A key success factor for change management is the establishment of a 'common language' to address the business process change and to set up an infrastructure for an efficient and effective application of this language. This is especially important for large organizations, like the defense sector. The language to describe the change of business processes must on one hand be easy to use because every employee of a company has to deal with it. On the other hand it must be very precise to avoid misunderstandings. Therefore, the use of graphical description methods, of modeling techniques, is recommended. Since the ARIS framework can be used to structure the content of all change management aspects, it can also be used to structure the required description methods, the language of change. Figure 6.4 shows various modeling methods, structured based on the ARIS framework. Organizational changes can be described using organizational charts, new activities can be explained by means of function trees, information needed or produced in a process can be described using entity relationship models (ERM), and changing deliverables may be presented using hierarchy diagrams. Finally, the entire process including all relations between the different views on the business process can be described using methods like event-driven process chains (EPC).

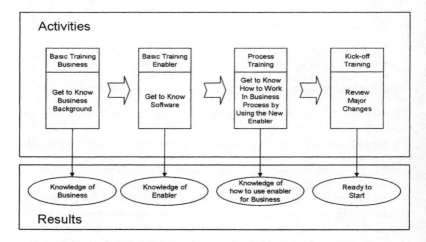

Figure 6.3: Business Process Oriented Training

Especially the definition of new process deliverables in the form of new market offerings should be done using appropriate graphical methods in order to understand the structure of those changes fully.[8]

The modeling methods used can vary depending on the target audience. Engineers may appreciate the use of very strict symbols like squares or diamonds, whereas manufacturing employees may prefer more 'tangible' and concrete symbols in the modeling language. During the enterprise specific definition of the language of change the move from one modeling technique to another has to be defined carefully.

The effective use of such modeling methods as a language for change depends heavily on the tools put in place in order to apply the methods. Those tools must be very user-friendly and ensure an efficient distribution of information across the organization. The use of Internet based technologies is therefore of high importance. However, it is not sufficient simply to publish information through the intranet or Internet. The tools infrastructure must also encourage a communication concerning possible change. Consequently an active modeling via the web is a requirement.

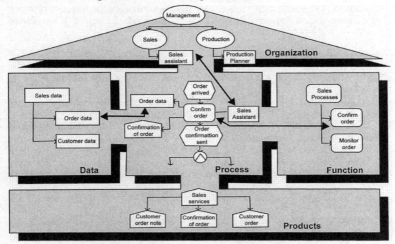

Figure 6.4: ARIS – Basis of a common language for change

The execution of the necessary training activities is in many cases the largest change management challenge for an organization. Very often thousands of people have to be trained in new business processes and new enablers such as application systems. Therefore concepts of distance learning using the Internet as an enabler becomes more and more important.[9] This concept reduces the logistical challenges tremendously and ensures a constant and consistent training quality.

NOTES

1. Scheer, A.-W., Abolhassan, F., Jost, W., Kirchmer, M.: Business Process Change Management – ARIS in Practice. Berlin, New York, and others 2003.
2. Jost, W., Scheer, A.-W.: Business Process Management: A Core Task for any Company Organization. In: Scheer, A.-W., Abolhassan, F., Jost, W., Kirchmer, M.: Business Process Excellence – ARIS in Practice. Berlin, New York, and others 2002, p. 33-43.
3. Spath, D., Baumeister, M., Barrho, T., Dill, C.: Change Management im Wandel. In: Industrie Management – Zeitschrift fuer industrielle Geschaeftsprozesse, 4/2001, p. 9-13.
4. Hammer, M., Stanton, S.: The Reengineering Revolution. Glasgow 1995

5. Scheer, A.-W.: Business Process Engineering. 2nd edition, Berlin, New York, and others 1994
6. Collins, J.: Good to Great – Why some companies make the leap and others don't. New York 2001.
7. Kirchmer, M.: Business Process Oriented Implementation of Standard Software – How to Achieve Competitive Advantage Efficiently and Effectively. 2nd edition, Berlin, New York and others 1999.
8. Elzina, D.J., Gulledge, T.R., Lee, C.-Y.: Business Engineering. Norwell 1999.
9. Kirchmer, M.: e-Business Processes – A Complete Lifecycle Management Approach. White Paper. Berwyn 2000.

BIBLIOGRAPHY

Collins, J.: Good to Great – Why some companies make the leap and others don't. New York 2001.

Elzina, D.J., Gulledge, T.R., Lee, C.-Y.: Business Engineering. Norwell 1999.

Hammer, M., Stanton, S.: The Reengineering Revolution. Glasgow 1995

IDS Scheer AG (editor): Business Process Management – ARIS Toolset Products. White Paper, Saarbruecken 02/2000.

Jost, W., Scheer, A.-W.: Business Process Management: A Core Task for any Company Organization. In: Scheer, A.-W., Abolhassan, F., Jost, W., Kirchmer, M.: Business Process Excellence – ARIS in Practice. Berlin, New York, and others 2002

Kirchmer, M., Brown, G., Heinzel, H.: Using SCOR and Other Reference Models for E-Business Process Networks. In: Scheer, A.-W., Abolhassan, F., Jost, W., Kirchmer, M.: Business Process Excellence – ARIS in Practice. Berlin, New York, and others 2002.

Kirchmer, M.: Business Process Oriented Implementation of Standard Software – How to Achieve Competitive Advantage Efficiently and Effectively. 2nd edition, Berlin, New York and others 1999.

Kirchmer, M., Scheer, A.-W.: Business Process Change Management – Key for Business Process Excellence. In: Scheer, A.-W., Abolhassan, F., Jost, W.,

Kirchmer, M.: Business Process Change Management – ARIS in Practice. Berlin, New York, and others 2003.

Kirchmer, M.: e-Business Processes – A Complete Lifecycle Management Approach. White Paper. Berwyn 2000.

Kirchmer, M.: Market- and Product-Oriented Definition of Business Processes. In: Elzina, D.J., Gulledge, T.R., Lee, C.-Y.: Business Engineering. Norwell 1999.

Kraemer, W., Mueller, M.: Virtuelle Corporate University – Executive Education Architecture and Knowledge Management. In: Scheer, A.-W. (Editor): Electronic Business und Knowledge Management – Neue Dimensionen fuer den Unternehmenserfolg. Heidelberg 1999.

Kraemer, W., Gallenstein, C., Sprendger, P.: Learning Management fuer Fuehrungskraefte. In: Industrie Management – Zeitschrift fuer industrielle Geschaeftsprozesse, 4/2001

Scheer, A.-W.: CIM – Computer Integrated Manufacturing. 3rd edition, Berlin, New York, and others 1994.

Scheer, A.-W.: Business Process Engineering. 2nd edition, Berlin, New York, and others 1994.

Scheer, A.-W.: ARIS – Business Process Frameworks. 2nd edition, Berlin, New York and others 1998.

Scheer, A.-W., Abolhassan, F., Jost, W., Kirchmer, M.: Business Process Excellence – ARIS in Practice. Berlin, New York, and others 2002.

Scheer, A.-W., Abolhassan, F., Jost, W., Kirchmer, M.: Business Process Change Management – ARIS in Practice. Berlin, New York, and others 2003.

Scheer, A.-W. (ed.): Electronic Business and Knowledge Management – Neue Dimensionen fuer den Unternehmenserfolg. Heidelberg 1999.

Scheer, A.-W.: ARIS – Business Process Modeling. 2nd edition, Berlin, New York and others 1998.

Spath, D., Baumeister, M., Barrho, T., Dill, C.: Change Management im Wandel. In: Industrie Management – Zeitschrift fuer industrielle Geschaeftsprozesse, 4/2001.

7. Establishing Process Ownership by Aligning SAP and DoD Business Processes[1]

David Bailey, Thomas Gulledge, and Georg Simon

INTRODUCTION

A common concern of DoD executives is that DoD business processes are not directly observable in Solution Architectures. For example, in a recent exchange the following was stated, 'if the Army's definition of the "supply management" process does not align with the SAP process, we are going to have unbelievable problems if we don't recognize that early'. The following was also noted, 'in the corporate world the Supply Chain Process includes the Distribution Process as a subset, not vice versa or as separate processes. SAP's definition of both is unclear'. This is a general problem with products like SAP, in that the reference business processes are contained in modules, while the actual business processes are cross-functional processes that flow across modules. With SAP, this apparent inconsistency is resolved late in the implementation process by defining cross-module test scenarios to support integration testing. This creates difficulty in assigning process owners, and usually results in defining module owners, such as finance, maintenance, transportation, etc. True process ownership should assign ownership to the cross-functional processes, just as the senior leaders have noted above. This chapter shows how the US Army can establish process ownership for Army core processes, while remaining consistent with SAP business process definitions. In short, we show how to map SAP processes to Army processes in the architecture, and establish business process ownership for both. The approach allows DoD executives to understand how DoD processes will be implemented in SAP, while simultaneously developing the cross-module scenarios that can be imposed on the implementation.

The US Army and Navy are implementing the SAP standard software solution. Their Solution Architectures were developed using objects from the SAP R/3 Reference Model. This reference model was developed for SAP to support their implementation methodology, which was known as Business Engineering. SAP's implementation methodology calls for the establishment of business process owners that align with the business process objects that are contained in the reference model. Consequently, the Single Army Logistics Enterprise (SALE) study recommends that the Army establish business process owners that align with the SAP business process objects. The recommendation has created discussions, since the SAP business process objects do not directly align with Army business processes. SAP business processes are typically associated with SAP modules such as human resources or financials, while Army business processes typically flow across modules. This chapter addresses the complexity and level of effort required to manipulate and use the SAP R/3 Reference Model to meet ERP architectural needs; i.e., defining business processes in terms that the customer can accept with some level of comfort.

In particular, the chapter addresses an issue that is critical to establishing true business process ownership when implementing the SAP standard software solution. The SAP business processes, as documented in the Army and Navy solution architectures, are directly aligned with the modules in the SAP solution. However, DoD business processes flow across modules and should be managed as end-to-end (E2E) business process scenarios. The Army and Navy Strategies, Architectures, and Standards Groups (SASGs) have been working this problem for the last five years, and have developed an approach to establishing process ownership and implementation control using what is known in the commercial literature as a 'Customer-Specific Reference Model'. This allows the implementing organization to simultaneously establish business process ownership in terms of customer-specific and SAP-specific business processes.

To illustrate the difficulties in documenting Army business processes, consider the following example, the Army process for Configured Load Processing. This business process flows not only across a number of SAP modules but in and out of several non-SAP components. This has led to much confusion, as Army managers find themselves unable to identify their business processes in the SAP software or the SALE architecture. Because Configured Load Processing is composed of activities contained within material management, transportation, financial, and other functional areas, a modular oriented process ownership structure is inappropriate for managing this process. It is possible to establish a process owner for Configured Load Processing, and Configured Load Processing can be configured in SAP, but Configured Load Processing is not a traditional SAP business process that is documented in the SAP Reference Model. Configured Load Processing is an Army-specific business process; hence, it must be documented in a Customer-Specific reference model.

A Customer-Specific Reference Model contains critical customer business processes, organized in E2E scenarios, to illustrate not only the process flow across SAP modules but across non-SAP components as well. Cross-module business processes map customer processes directly to SAP Reference model processes, enabling the establishment of clear process ownership. These scenarios also allow for the management of the implementation in accordance with business processes that are easily understood by the customer. This results in a two-way mapping of business process ownership. There is ownership in terms of the E2E cross-module scenarios, as well as the traditional SAP modular process orientation. Additionally, a Customer-Specific Reference Model enables an organization to understand how a planned SAP implementation will relate and interoperate with non-SAP components as required by the cross-functional scenarios.

A useful by-product of the approach that is described in this chapter is that the E2E scenarios become the test scenarios that are executed in the integration-testing phase of the SAP implementation. If the implementing organization has documented its critical business processes that flow across the SAP modules, then the ability of implementation consultants[2] to demonstrate the capability of the SAP software to execute these E2E scenarios to customer expectations becomes the standard by which success can be measured.

This chapter shows how the Customer Specific Reference Model is derived to support an SAP implementation. In addition, this paper addresses how the Customer-Specific Reference Model 'maps' SAP processes to organizational-specific processes. The chapter also provides a strategy for aligning SAP processes with the organizational-specific business processes that are described in the Customer-Specific Reference Model, and makes specific recommendations for the US Army Logistics SAP implementation. The examples demonstrated within will show how the Customer-Specific Reference Model is used to ensure that an E2E solution is tested and realized in complex SAP implementation like that in the US Army and the US Navy.

The examples used to illustrate the use of a Customer-Specific Reference have been taken from the Navy ERP convergence effort, since the E2E scenarios for the Army are still under development. The SASG is working aggressively to complete these scenarios, with an objective to have rough drafts in the May–June (2004) period.

DERIVING A CUSTOMER-SPECIFIC REFERENCE MODEL

The development of an enterprise resource planning (ERP) Architecture using the SAP R/3 Reference Model requires a significant effort to align the modular orientation of the SAP software with the value-chain oriented cross-functional business processes that are the output of a fully configured and integrated SAP solution. The reference model has a modular orientation and the layering of the models does not always imply a hierarchy or decomposition. ERP process architectures are based on enterprise-level value chains that are hierarchically decomposed into various levels of detail and down to a transaction level. Figure 7.1 is a depiction of a high-level value chain.

Each business process object at the enterprise level decomposes into another value chain that represents the level 2 business processes in the SAP R/3 Reference Model. Figure 7.2 depicts the level-2 decomposition of the Financial Management value chain in Figure 7.1.

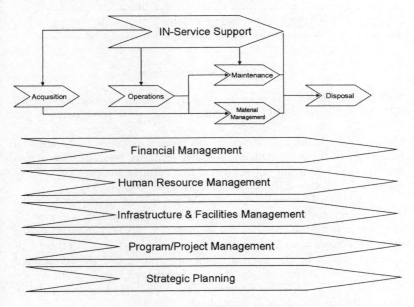

Figure 7.1: ERP Value Chain Architecture

This model depicts the business processes that are supported by SAP in the Financial Management area. One limitation of this representation is that the hierarchical decomposition presents a function-oriented depiction of the Financial Management business processes. This is consistent with the function-oriented depictions that are provided in SAP Solution Maps. The decomposition of the Financial Management business process does not show how the details of the Financial Management sub-processes relate to the other value chains within the architecture.

However, the representation is still a desired model for purposes of demonstrating the business processes that are executed and scoped within an

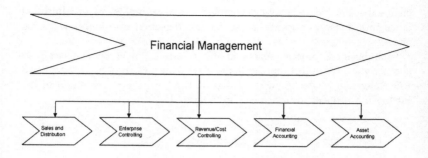

Figure 7.2: Financial Management Value Chain

SAP module. In fact, this example precisely describes the assertion that the SAP R/3 Reference Model has a modular orientation. However, in reality this is not the way that business is conducted inside of organizations. Organizations do not limit their business process execution to the artificial boundaries of the SAP modules. Business processes typically flow across modules (and even in and out of SAP) as E2E business process scenarios. We collectively call these E2E business processes, the 'Scenario View'.

This additional scenario view should be created to depict how the organization actually conducts business. In this sense, the E2E scenarios are very similar to the test scenarios that are created to support integration testing in the final stages of an SAP implementation. Our assertion is that these E2E scenarios should be documented in the architecture and owned/managed throughout the implementation process. Examples of E2E scenarios are provided in Table 7.1. These scenarios relate to US Army Logistics, and they are described in more detail in Appendix A.

The scenarios in Table 7.1 are comprised of SAP and non-SAP business process objects. All of the objects (SAP and non-SAP) should be documented in the Single Army Logistics Enterprise Architecture. Hence, these E2E scenarios flow across the architecture, similar to the SAP concept of an x-App. The complete documentation and mapping of the scenarios in Table 7.1 defines the Customer-Specific Reference Model for Logistics. These detailed processes represent the way that the Army does its business, so we assert that the Army should establish a process owner for each of these business processes. This does not preclude having module-oriented process owners for SAP, and some business process owners may have multiple assignments; i.e., by module and cross-functional process.

US Army Logistics E2E Scenarios

- Order Fulfillment
- Unserviceable Reparable Retrograde
- Reporting/Disposition of Excess
- Push Packages
- Configured Load Processing
- Modification Work Order Processing
- Safety of Use Notification/Processing
- Quality Deficiency Report Processing
- RFID/AIT Enabled Distribution Management
- Basic National/Tactical Supply Operations (SSF via SAP)
- National Maintenance Management Processing
- Contractor Logistics Support
- Task Force Reorganization
- Battlefield Loss/Major Item Replacement
- Stockage Determination
- Issue of Pre-positioned War Reserve Stocks
- Introduction of New Equipment into the Army

Table 7.1: Example of E2E Business Process Scenarios[3]

The Customer Specific Reference Model is partially constructed from objects in the SAP Reference Model, so there is a complete mapping of the Army processes to the SAP processes. The derivation of a specific E2E scenario from a solution architecture is presented in the next section.

Deriving the E2E Scenario

The E2E scenarios are derived from existing level-3 processes in the SAP Reference Model, as they are defined in the business process architecture. The business process objects are arranged sequentially to reflect the true end-to-end customer-specific business process. We have created an example scenario how the E2E scenario flows across SAP modules. Figure 7.3 depicts a US Navy Breakdown Maintenance scenario that includes 28 level-4 processes and crosses six different modules of SAP. Figure 7.4 provides an enlargement of a segment of the same E2E business process.

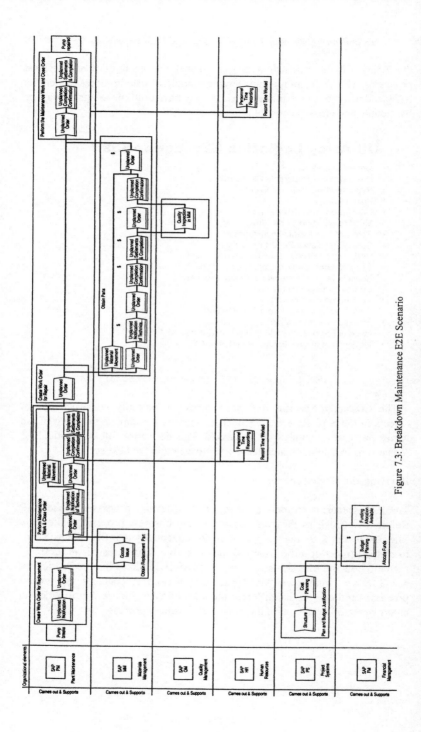

Figure 7.3: Breakdown Maintenance E2E Scenario

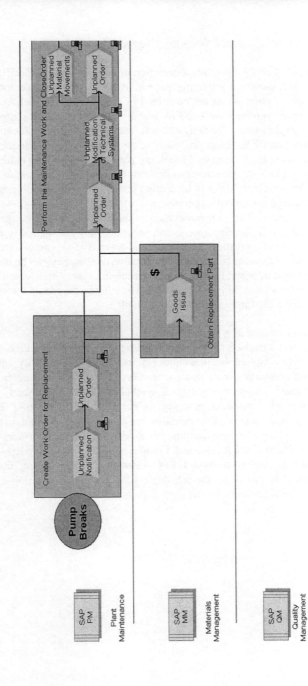

Figure 7.4: Breakdown Maintenance E2E Scenario Detail

Figures 7.3 and 7.4 provide a depiction of a key customer-specific business process that does not explicitly appear in the SAP reference model. It is comprised of objects that are contained in the reference model, but they are 're-arranged' to reflect the true E2E scenario as viewed by the customer. This example explains why the DoD customer has so much trouble identifying key customer-specific business processes in the SAP Reference Model; i.e., they do not exist in the Reference Model, but they must be derived external of the reference model. It also demonstrates that by creating value-chains scenarios SAP functional activities can be unified into a true representation of the way the configured system will operate.

In a typical SAP implementation, these E2E scenarios are ad-hoc developed late in the implementation process. They are manually derived to support integration testing. The Army and Navy SASGs are working hard to derive these scenarios prior to implementation so that they can be understood, managed, and imposed by the Executive Steering Committee as test scenarios that must be successfully executed prior to the acceptance of the configured solution from the implementation consultants.

Additional Details at a Lower Level
Levels-3 and 4 of the SAP Reference Model are Event-driven Process Chains (EPCs) with implied business process interfaces. Graphically the models begin and end with events that are repeated in the various models to which they interface. The process interface symbol that would graphically show the link to the other business processes is not included in the SAP Reference Model, so the links across modules are not clearly defined in the SAP solution. In order to correct this, all business process interfaces must be manually added to the level-3 and 4 models and linked appropriately.

Figure 7.5 depicts a level-4 EPC before and after adding the process interfaces. The model on the left depicts the before the addition of process interfaces and the model on the right depicts the after state.

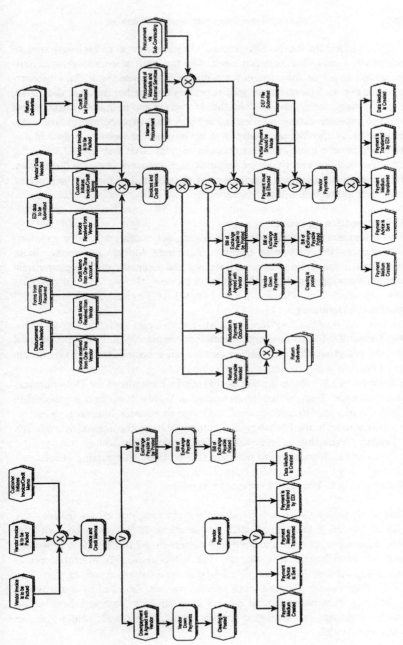

Figure 7.5: Level-4 EPC Comparison

This addition to the SAP Reference Model is critical to facilitate smooth transitions among business processes. The business process interfaces must be added to all of the models for both the SAP events and the customer-specific events. The customer specific events add further detail in describing how the final configured solution should operate and help both management and the implementation team understand how SAP will operate relative to the organizations specific requirements at the business process level. In addition to descriptive events, custom interfaces to both SAP and non-SAP can be added to indicate exactly where in the business process flow interfaces must be designed and executed. All links must be validated relative to the business processes at levels-3 and 4.

Recommended Approach

The discussion in the previous section suggests a straightforward approach that derives the Customer Specific Reference Model, documents these processes in the architecture, and defines and manages the integration test scenarios throughout the implementation process. Hence, the Army Process Owners, supported by Business Area Leads, ERP Team SMEs and the SASG must do the following:

- Create the Customer-Specific Reference Model by fully developing and documenting the E2E scenarios that have been identified within the DoD.
- Develop E2E scenarios that could then be customized for DoD business processes. Test the scenario integration points down to the transaction level inside of the architecture and inside of Solution Manager.
- Formulate a methodology for communicating the approach with the senior leadership, program offices, and project teams.
- Use the E2E scenarios to facilitate E2E business blueprinting events.

Relationship to Business Process Ownership

This section addresses a critical part of the planning process by defining the role of process owners in an ERP environment. It also describes how the process owners relate to the SAP and customer-specific business processes that are described in this chapter. The establishment of the appropriate ownership relationships is a critical step in establishing a project plan. The section begins with a definition of process owners, followed by a discussion on the role of business process owners in an ERP environment. Finally, the chapter addresses problems that specifically relate to the Customer-Specific Reference Model.

Process Owners in a Private Sector Environment

Process Owner (Industry Definition) – The business representative (user) responsible for engineering the business process. The process owner must be at a level senior enough to ensure authority over the business process and its interfaces.

A detailed discussion is provided by Keen and Knapp (1995).

Process owner is the term used to identify the individual who is assigned responsibility for a process and accorded the authority needed to fulfill that responsibility. Authority and accountability for processes, because they are defined in terms of parts of a process functional area, department, activity and tend to be highly fragmented in most companies. Customer procurement, for example, is initiated by a customer order and progresses through production scheduling, manufacturing operations, distribution, accounts receivables, and finance. Authority and accountability are distributed among the respective functional units. A process owner would exercise responsibility for the customer procurement process, end-to-end, employing influence or management authority to ensure its coordination.

The concept of process owner, being relatively new, examples in practice are few. What it implies is the matching of authority and accountability in a cross-functional environment. Three practical approaches include (1) assigning process ownership to an individual within the existing functional structure, (2) designating as process owner a senior corporate manager, and (3) organizing around business processes, with the process owner being equivalent to a line executive and vice versa. The first leaves the existing authority-accountability relationship intact and introduces a new role, a type of coordinator who must negotiate with the functional areas. The second approach co-opts existing authority by transferring responsibility for a function to an individual who possesses organizational clout and can command, not just negotiate. The third approach supplants functional structure by developing authority and accountability around processes directly.

Most DoD ERP implementations have selected the first option for process ownership.

Process Owners in an ERP Environment

As described above, ERP software is aligned with business processes. The software enables business process execution while simultaneously achieving cross-functional process integration. In this environment, the role of the process owner is more significant, since cross-functional processes span organizational, political, and budgetary boundaries.

One ongoing discussion in the management literature concerns the role of line management process owners versus systems/IT managers in ERP implementation. The consensus is that both are important, but they support the implementation process with different foci and timing. The business process owners are dominant throughout the implementation process, while in the latter stages the technologists play a significant supporting role. The process owner approves all significant decisions about business process implementation and scope. These decisions bound the domain of the technologies. Since the technologists have historically dominated the systems implementation process, this overt shift in power has revolutionized the way we think about requirements definition, design specification, and implementation. The process owner:

- Understands how organizational plans link to the business process, and is accountable for any process-related performance measures.
- Intimately understands the process, and is capable and enthusiastic about making decisions that impact the way that work is executed within the owned business processes.
- Resolves any internal disputes about business process standardization.
- Makes decisions about project scope by defining and documenting which business processes will be enabled by the ERP software.
- Manages the implementation business case and project plan, trading-off cost, benefits, and schedule while achieving organizational objectives.
- Maintains business process configuration control, and approves all changes in business processes that are required to align processes with the ERP software while minimizing any software customization.
- Leads (or play a major supporting role) in the implementation project within their domain.
- Negotiates with and manages IT Department support within the domain.
- Interfaces with corporate leadership to be sure that process integration with other process owners is being realized.

The DoD Environment

Business process ownership in the DoD environment will by necessity have a different meaning. The process owners are 'Corporate-Level' owners, and the Project Program Offices represent single implementation occurrences. Hence, although the program is the recipient of the software solution, the program manager will not have final authority to resolve all process-related issues. Since the software will eventually be implemented on other organizations, the idea is to standardize as much as possible across programs. Hence, an individual program may have to make compromises on some business process issues. The business process owners are more like corporate executives who are making decisions about how the business processes will be implemented across multiple plants or divisions. In this case, the usual position of the executive is to standardize the implementation as much as possible in order to maintain consistent business rules and practices, while at the same time minimizing problems relating to supply, maintenance, asset tracking, configuration management, and other logistics-related processes

The SALE study recommended process owners that map directly to the SAP modules. The process areas were pulled directly from the architecture. For resolving questions that relate to specific SAP configuration problems in the associated SAP modules, the recommended process owners are appropriate. Through a mapping process, Army Executives reduced the recommended process areas to a smaller subset. This mapping is indicated in Figure 7.6.

Business Process Areas Crosswalk

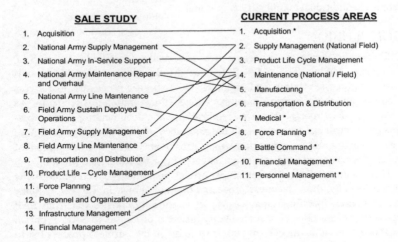

Figure 7.6: Business Process Cross Walk Between Current Army and SAP Processes

There is nothing wrong with the approach in Figure 7.6. There can be arguments about the mappings, but Figure 7.6 does align SAP business process objects with Army business process areas. However, Figure 7.6 does not include Army E2E business process that flow across modules. That is, it is impossible to identify the cross-functional processes in Table 7.1 in this mapping approach.

This leaves the Army with several approaches for moving forward:

- Use a business process owner assignment similar to that in Figure 7.6. This will work, but it does not provide direct ownership over the business processes in Table 7.1.
- Assign owners to the processes in Table 7.1, which establishes business process control in terms of E2E Army processes.
- Use a business process owner assignment similar to that in Figure 7.6 but assign them responsibility for the E2E processes in Table 7.1. This option assigns responsibility for cross-functional business processes without increasing the number of 'process owners'.

Options 2 or 3 are not necessarily more complicated than option 1, since the processes in Table 7.1 will have to be derived and documented, and this is independent of process ownership. Table 7.1 defines the integration test scenarios, and each integration test scenario must have an owner, so in this sense, the additional complexity is minimal.

CONCLUSION

DoD-specific business processes are not easily identified in the SAP Reference Model. The SAP Reference Model defines and documents business processes within SAP modules. DoD-specific processes flow across modules, and they are prime candidates for SAP integration test scenarios. As such, it is the Process Owner's responsibility for documenting these cross-functional business processes with the assistance of the SASG, Business Area Leads and the SAP project implementation teams. The documentation of these E2E scenarios is known as a Customer-Specific Reference Model.

The Customer-Specific Reference Model specifically documents Army processes; e.g., those business processes that are shown in Table 7.1. Since the Customer-Specific Reference Model is partially constructed from SAP business process objects, it maps Army business processes to SAP. From an SAP point of view, the current task is to stabilize the business process list in Table 7.1, and to define and document those processes.

From an Army business process ownership perspective, the alignment is more subtle. Army executives are concerned that they do not see Army business processes in SAP. The creation of mappings from Army business process areas to SAP business process objects (Figure 7.6) does not solve this problem. However, there is a solution. The Army can assign ownership to the processes in Table 7.1. Since the processes in Table 7.1 will be documented in the SALE architecture, this establishes ownership over Army-specific processes. The approach is simplified because cross ownership is provided across Table 7.1 and Figure 7.6. That is, the owners of the processes in right hand panel of Figure 7.6 would be owners of the cross-functional processes in Table 7.1. This establishes the ownership of Army-specific business processes and specifically links those processes to SAP business process objects. This addresses the immediate concern of the senior executives. If ownership is established, then the Army has direct control of Army business processes as they are configured and tested in SAP.

NOTES

1. The authors thank Mr. Wael Hafez, Mr. Forrest Malcomb, and Dr. Carsten Svennson for comments on an earlier version of this paper. We also thank Mr. Forrest Malcomb and Mr. James Kipers for the contribution of Appendix A.
2. In DoD parlance, the implementation consultants are sometimes called 'integrators'.
3. These processes are only examples and are not meant to be complete. The Army SASG is still vetting these processes, and additional processes may be added and others may be deleted.

BIBLIOGRAPHY

Keen, Peter G.W. and Ellen M. Knapp, Business Processes. Boston: Harvard Business School Press, 1995.

APPENDIX A: US ARMY LOGISTICS E2E SCENARIOS

1. ORDER FULFILLMENT:

a) Definition: A deployed customer (company/battalion level) orders a part (DLA managed item) to support the repair of a piece of unit equipment. The requirement is recorded and passed to the national level for fill. The part is shipped from a national level depot; processed through the supporting tactical supply support activity/forward distribution point and issued to the customer. Transactions, including status changes, are properly recorded in all supply systems. Required transactions are provided to supporting financial and in-transit visibility / asset visibility systems.

b) Possible branches/sequels:
  i. Request initiated by on-board sensor (CLOE/PSMRS).
  ii. Request is initiated via Interactive Electronic Technical Manual (IETM).
  iii. Item management in non-Army (DLA).
  iv. Item is on hand at SSA/FDP directly supporting the customer.
  v. Item available at SSA/FDP not directly supporting the customer.
  vi. Request is from USMC BN (joint support).
  vii. Request is initiated by manual screen input.

c) Key integrations items:
  i. Basic order processing flow. Possible routes:
    1. Unit to SSA to AMC, then through the hub to DLA.
    2. Unit to SSA to hub to AMC or DLA.
    3. Unit to SSA to hub to AMC then DLA.
    4. Unit to AMC, material release order (MRO) back to SSA, others to DLA via hub or direct.
    5. Unit to DLA, MRO's back to SSA.
    6. Role of DAAS in all this?

  ii. Prioritization of requests for issue (highest priority/oldest date versus first ordered ... how to do this in SAP?).
  iii. Serial number tracking for special programs, e.g. Unique Identification tracking, COMSEC, etc.
  iv. Financial interfaces, to include support for non-Army (e.g., USMC).
  v. Critical items status reported to C2 system.

      vi. Should the system support multiple NSN's/part numbers being ordered on the same transaction?

     vii. DLMS replacement for MILSTRIP/MILSTAMP standards.

d) Key Participants (Organizations and Systems we must interact with to properly work scenario):
    i. GCSS-Army
    ii. LMP
   iii. PLM+
   iv. DLA (BSM)
    v. TRANSCOM
   vi. DFAS

2. UNSERVICEABLE/REPARABLE RETROGRADE.

a. Definition: A direct support maintenance activity must replace a reparable component. The replacement item must be ordered and filled in accordance with scenario 1 above. The unserviceable item must be turned in to the supporting SSA/FDP and retrograded through to the appropriate activity authorized to repair the item. Transactions, including status changes, are posted in all systems. Required transactions are provided to supporting financial and in transit visibility / asset visibility systems.

b. Possible branches/sequels:
    i. Unserviceable part available for turn-in within prescribed timeframe.
    ii. Unserviceable part turned in after prescribed timeframe.
   iii. Unserviceable part not available for turn-in.
   iv. The repair activity is an installation-level maintenance activity rather than a national level depot.
    v. Unserviceable/reparable item is DS/RX.

c. Key integrations items:
    i. Automatic routing of unserviceable retrograde (how to know where the item should be sent for repair?).
    ii. Exchange pricing business rules.
   iii. Serial number tracking (contact memory buttons).
   iv. Retrograde ITV (including RFID)
    v. DLMS replacement for MILSTRIP/MILSTAMP standards.

d. **Key Participants** (Organizations and Systems we must interact with to properly work scenario):
    i.   GCSS-Army
    ii. LMP
    iii. PLM+
    iv. TRANSCOM
    v.   DFAS

3. REPORTING/DISPOSITION OF EXCESS

a. **Definition:** The quantity of an item on hand at a tactical SSA/FDP fully meets the stockage requirement locally. A customer unit turns in some of the same item placing the SSA/FDP in an overstocked condition. The excess items are reported to the national level manager/management system and a disposition decision is made to ship the items to another storage activity. The material release order is produced, the SSA contacts the supporting Transportation activity to arrange for transportation, and the supplies are shipped to and receipted at the designated storage activity. Transactions are produced to meet the requirements of all financial and in-transit visibility/asset visibility systems.

b. **Possible branches/sequels:**
    i.   Item is excess to the overall requirement and is directed to disposal.
    ii.   Item is on the 'automatic return item list' (ARIL); excess reporting is not needed to initiate the excess disposition process.
    iii. Item not on hand at time of customer order so request passed to national level. Subsequently items are turned in by another customer as excess and are picked up at the SSA.
    iv.   All requests for the excess item are routed to that SSA until stocks are drawn down.

c. **Key integrations items:**
    i.   Basic flow of excess reporting transactions? (SSA to MMC? To National? To DLA?)
    ii.   Automatic reporting of and shipment of excess (functionality not available in R/3?).
    iii. Automatic shipment or ARIL items (functionality not available in R/3?).
    iv.   Cancellation of excess dues-in based on turn-ins received at the local level.

    v. DLMS replacement for MILSTRIP/MILSTAMP standards.

d. **Key Participants** (Organizations and Systems we must interact with to properly work scenario):
- i. GCSS-Army
- ii. LMP
- iii. PLM+
- iv. DLA
- v. TRANSCOM
- vi. DFAS

4. PUSH PACKAGES

a. **Definition:** A unit is deploying to a military operation. The national manager 'pushes' operations-specific items (e.g., cold-weather uniforms, chemical protective suits) to the supporting SSA. In-transit visibility is provided throughout the process and the receiving SSA/FDP receives automatic notification that the items are being provided. All supporting financial and in-transit transactions are created and systems are updated. Status changes are reported throughout the process.

b. **Possible branches/sequels:**
- i. Push package is intended for a specific unit rather than the supporting SSA.
- ii. Total Package Fielding (TPF) push for a major item including repair parts for stockage at the unit and SSA level.
- iii. Receipt not due-in push package arrives at SSA.

c. **Key integrations items** that need to be worked via this E2E Scenario:
- i. Release authority for push packages including coordination with gaining commands.
- ii. Gaining unit must have automated visibility of what is being pushed so they do not order the same items and clog the distribution pipeline.
- iii. In-transit visibility for push packages.

d. **Key Participants** (Organizations and Systems we must interact with to properly work scenario):
- i. GCSS-Army
- ii. LMP
- iii. PLM+
- iv. TRANSCOM
- v. DFAS

5. CONFIGURED LOAD PROCESSING

a. **Definition:**   To support a specific military operation a theater commander directs the assembly of a configured load of hot-weather related items.   The package is to be assigned a specific NSN/part number. A new NSN/part number is created and populated throughout the system. Customers requisition the package based on the new NSN. The item manager directs release.   The items are shipped and all appropriate supply, financial and in-transit visibility/total asset visibility transactions are created and properly recorded throughout the system. The packages are received at the supporting SSA/FDP, processed and released to the intended units.

b. **Possible branches/sequels:**
>   i. Before all items in the configured load can be assembled in full quantity, the theater commander directs that the packages be pushed to the units. Package is shipped with shortages.
>   ii. Customers are blocked from requisitioning the item; it can only be provided on a push-basis at the direction of the national manager.
>   iii. Package contains items substituted for other items not available at time of shipment.

c. **Key integrations items:**
>   i. Proper billing.
>   ii. How to account for shortages in the packages?
>   iii. How to account for items shipped directly to the customer unit when initial shortages become available?

d. **Key Participants:**
>   i. GCSS-Army
>   ii. LMP
>   iii. PLM+
>   iv. DFAS
>   v. TRANSCOM

6. MODIFICATION WORK ORDER PROCESSING

a. **Definition:** A required maintenance action requiring specific parts must be accomplished on a specific vehicle type across the Army inventory. The MWO kit is ordered as an entity by a unique part number. The parts request from the maintenance activity is received and processed at the SSA/FDP and the parts are issued. The maintenance activity records the receipt of the parts. Job orders are opened to conduct the application of the MWO. Parts are issued to the mechanics and recorded as used on the specific job. Once the work has been completed the work order is closed and the work reported to the national maintenance system. In addition the equipment record for each item is updated to reflect the application of the MWO.

b. **Possible branches/sequels:**
   i. The parts needed for the MWO are assembled into a kit at the national level and are push-resupplied to the SSA/FDP level. Work is performed at the direct support unit level.
   ii. The item must be sent to the supporting installation or special repair activity to have the MWO applied.
   iii. Applying the MWO changes the identity of the major item (NSN change, LIN change).
   iv. Applying the MWO changes the identity of the component (NSN change).

c. **Key integrations items**:
   i. How will units be notified of MWO requirements?
   ii. How will MWO accomplishments be tracked?
   iii. NSN and LIN changes properly recorded in all systems.
   iv. Maintenance man-hours recorded and charged.
   v. Serial number tracking updated.

d. **Key Participants** (Organizations and Systems we must interact with to properly work scenario):
   i. GCSS-Army
   ii. LMP
   iii. PLM+
   iv. DFAS
   v. TRANSCOM

7. **SAFETY OF USE NOTIFICATION/PROCESSING**

a. **Definition:**   An aircraft crash investigation reveals that there is a systemic defect in a component of the helicopter. As a result, all helicopters of that model must have the part removed and replaced with an improved part. A SOUM (Safety of Use Message) is issued. The improved part is designed by the manufacturer, tested and accepted by the Army. A new part number/NSN is assigned. All logistics systems are updated with the new part information. The appropriate IETM is updated. The national manager procures and stocks sufficient quantities of the new item to outfit all aircraft. Parts are push-issued to the SSA's supporting the affected aviation units.   Parts are ordered by the supporting aircraft maintenance activity, issued and installed on the aircraft. Completion of the maintenance work order is reported via the maintenance reporting system to the national level. The national inventory manager also automatically directs the turn-in of all of the defective part that are currently in stock anywhere in the system. Material release orders are cut, items are dropped from inventory and are turned in to the supporting disposal activity.

b. **Key integrations items:**
  i.   Critical information passed to C2 system.
  ii. Financial transactions.

c. **Key Participants** (Organizations and Systems we must interact with to properly work scenario):
  i.   GCSS-Army
  ii. LMP
  iii. PLM+
  iv. DFAS
  v.   TRANSCOM

9. QUALITY DEFICIENCY REPORT PROCESSING

a. **Definition:** A customer unit orders an item. The order is processed completely through the system. The item is released from the national level and shipped to the SSA/FDP directly supporting the customer. The supporting SSA/FDP receives the item and releases it to the ordering unit. Upon receipt in the ordering unit it is noted that there is a quantity discrepancy (e.g., ordered 10, quantity shipped indicated as 10, actual quantity received is 7). The using unit enters the discrepancy into the automated system. The appropriate supply and financial discrepancy transactions are created and reported to the shipping activity. In addition, the discrepancy report generates a new candidate supply request for the missing quantity (customer action required to process the order to ensure the requirement is still valid).

b. **Possible branches/sequels:**

  i.   QDR if for item received for stockage at SSA rather than customer unit.
  ii. Quantity is correct but item is damaged or destroyed or has a maintenance defect.

c. **Key integrations items:**
  i.   EDI formats for QDR reporting?

   ii. Accepting turn-ins of QDR item and granting of any credit due.
   iii. Proper recording of financial transactions.
   iv. Warranty considerations.

d. Key Participants (Organizations and Systems we must interact with to properly work scenario):
   i. GCSS-Army
   ii. LMP
   iii. PLM+
   iv. DFAS
   v. DLA

9. RFID/AIT/MTS ENABLED DISTRIBUTION MANAGEMENT

a. Definition: Supply/distribution operations are conducted in such a manner as to provide accurate and continually updated in-transit visibility. Shipments between various nodes in the distribution system are tagged with RFID devices. Interrogators are placed at key points in the distribution system and read information from shipments bearing RFID devices. Information read is passed throughout all systems to provide visibility on the location and expected delivery date of orders. Movement Tracking System (MTS) reports location of transportation assets and their cargo. Information from RFID technology devices is used to automatically create transactions which feed supply and critical transportation systems.

b. Possible branches/sequels:
   i. An incoming part must be located in the distribution system and redirected to another location.

c. Key integrations items:
   i. AIT Technology standards and ITV data standards.
   ii. Critical information reported to C2 system.
   iii. Automatic processing of supply transactions based on RFID feeds (do we want to do this – doctrine?).
   iv. DLMS replacement for MILSTRIP/MILSTAMP standards.
   v. Movement Tracking System (MTS).

d. Key Participants (Organizations and Systems we must interact with to properly work scenario):
   i. GCSS-Army
   ii. LMP
   iii. PLM+

    iv. DLA
    v. TRANSCOM

10. BASIC NATIONAL/TACTICAL SUPPLY OPERATIONS INTERACTION

a. **Definition:** Routine supply actions are accomplished effectively across all components of the enterprise. Inventory adjustments at the SSA/FDP level are automatically reported to the national level. Material Release Denials create appropriate adjustment documents and re-establish the unfilled quantity of the order. Part number/NSN and other catalog changes are processed accurately and all systems are updated correctly. Inventory adjustment reports create inventory count requests and systems are updated based on the results of the count.

b. **Key integrations items:**
    i. Serial number tracking.
    ii. HAZMAT management.
    iii. Shelf-life management.
    iv. Use of RFID/AIT.
    v. Warehouse denials, including re-establishment of original requirement.
    vi. Catalog data changes.
    vii. Inventory results, adjustments, etc.

c. **Key Participants** (Organizations and Systems we must interact with to properly work scenario):
    i. GCSS-Army
    ii. LMP
    iii. PLM+
    iv. DFAS
    v. DLA

11. NATIONAL MAINTENANCE MANAGEMENT PROCESSING

a. **Definition:** The national level maintenance manager for an item has designated a tactical level maintenance activity as a repair source for a specific quantity. Unserviceable items are received at the SSA supporting the maintenance activity and are automatically released to the maintenance activity for repair up to the quantity authorized by the national manager. All parts requests, man-hour reports and job order status is reported to the national maintenance manager. The maintenance activity returns the item in serviceable condition to the SSA/FDP where it is receipted for and placed in inventory as issuable. Once that approved quantity has been repaired all future unserviceable receipts are retrograded to an SSA / FDP supporting a still-active maintenance repair program for that item.

b. **Possible branches/sequels:**
   i. Item is sent to maintenance but is unable to be repaired ('washout'). The carcass is retrograded/sent to disposal.
   ii. Supporting maintenance facility is backlogged and cannot accept any more job orders. Item still requires repair. How do we automatically identify back-up maintenance support activity and redirect the item?

c. **Key integrations items** that need to be worked via E2E Scenario:
   i. How will maintenance activities be notified that they are authorized to repair items under the national maintenance management system (i.e., how will this work in SAP?).
   ii. How will SSA be notified where to send items for repair?

d. **Key Participants** (Organizations and Systems we must interact with to properly work scenario):
   i. GCSS-Army
   ii. LMP
   iii. PLM+
   iv. DFAS
   v. TRANSCOM

12. CONTRACTOR LOGISTICS SUPPORT

a. **Definition:** A new system is being supported via Contractor Logistics Support. A using unit orders a part to repair an inoperative system. The item ordered is stocked by the contractor only (not stocked in Army inventory). The supply request is entered at the unit level and is processed. All supply and financial transactions are created and posted in the appropriate systems. All status transactions, including those coming from the contractor, are provided. All in-transit visibility/asset visibility systems are updated according to the same standards as for standard supply-system items.

b. **Possible branches/sequels:**
   i. Part is contractor owned but is consigned to the supporting SSA for stockage.
   ii. A one time authorization is given to purchase an item locally that is normally found within the Army inventory. One that is normally carried on the Army's stock number catalog. Note:

in SARSS, the wholesale level would authorize the request to be purchase locally one time with a DIC AE1 w/ CP, CW, DA in RP 65–66.

   iii. Part requires maintenance work by the CLS contractor.

c. **Key integrations items** that need to be worked via this E2E Scenario:

     i. Standards/formats for exchange of information between contractor's system and government system?

    ii. Information that must be exchanged between contractor's system and government system?

  iii. Warranty issues.

  iv. Financial transactions.

   v. Critical items status reported to C2 system.

d. **Key Participants** (Organizations and Systems we must interact with to properly work scenario):

     i. GCSS-Army

    ii. LMP

  iii. PLM+

  iv. DFAS

   v. TRANSCOM

13. TASK ORGANIZATION

a. **Definition:** A company is released from its parent battalion and attached to another battalion. The new battalion is supported by a different SSA/FDP. A transaction is processed to reflect the new supporting SSA/FDP and the effective date of the change. The new location automatically updates all records in the ERP and supporting systems. All open supply requests must be redirected automatically to the new SSA/FDP. Items not yet shipped will be shipped to the new location automatically. Items already in-transit will be automatically diverted automatically within the distribution system.

b. **Possible branches/sequels:**

     i. Company is split into platoons and each platoon is attached to a different battalion in a different geographic location. Each platoon has parts for its organic equipment due-in.

c. **Key integrations items** that need to be worked via this E2E Scenario:

     i. How to determine/report readiness for unit which is split into parts and deployed to multiple locations?

    ii. Financial billing.

    iii. Unit addresses (ship to, bill to, etc.).
    iv. Maintain and transfer dues-in, or re-establish requirement at new location?
    v. Retrograde and maintenance support.

d. Key Participants (Organizations and Systems we must interact with to properly work scenario):
    i. GCSS-Army
    ii. LMP
    iii. PLM+
    iv. TRANSCOM
    v. DFAS
    vi. DLA

14. BATTLEFIELD LOSS/MAJOR ITEM REPLACEMENT

a. Definition: A deployed unit's vehicle is destroyed and must be replaced. The loss is reported through the C2 system. In addition, the equipment is inspected and evaluated by a mechanic who confirms the replacement is required. The request is passed from the C2 system to the logistics system. The item is requested, authorizations and on-hand balances are checked and a replacement item issued from nationally owned inventory. The item is released from the national storage location and shipped to the SSA/FDP supporting the requesting unit. The item is received at the SSA/FDP. If the equipment is not in a ready-to-issue condition it is job ordered to maintenance for necessary work. The item is then issued to the customer. The customer's property record is updated and the item is added to the maintenance system at the unit and direct support level. The receipt of the item is also reported to the national level where authorization/balance systems are updated accordingly. All required transactions for supporting financial and in-transit visibility/asset visibility systems are updated.

b. Key integrations items that need to be worked via this E2E Scenario:
    i. TBD
    ii. TBD

c. Key Participants (Organizations and Systems we must interact with to properly work scenario):
    i. GCSS-Army
    ii. LMP
    iii. PLM+
    iv. DLA
    v. DFAS

vi.   TRANSCOM

15. STOCKAGE DETERMINATION

a.   **Definition:** A USAR supply unit that operates an SSA/FDP is deployed to a theater of operations. The unit deploys with no stocks in the SSA/FDP. The theater commander provides the units that will be supported by the SSA/FDP. The national level is notified of the deployment of the unit and a recommended stockage level. The location and support relationship of the SSA/FDP is entered and all appropriate systems/records are updated (i.e., DODAAC, Finance, etc.). The commander reviews the stockage recommendations and accepts them. The stockage levels are recorded and supplies are pushed from the national level to meet the requirement. All appropriate supply and financial transactions are created and recorded. All in-transit visibility and total asset visibility systems are continuously updated.

b.   **Key integrations items** that need to be worked via this E2E Scenario:
  i.   TBD
  ii.   TBD

c.   **Key Participants** (Organizations and Systems we must interact with to properly work scenario):
  i.   GCSS-Army
  ii.   LMP
  iii.   PLM+

16. ISSUE OF PREPOSITIONED WAR RESERVE STOCKS

a.   **Definition:** A unit deploys to an operational theater. Upon arrival in the theater the unit is issued equipment and parts to support that equipment. Issues of equipment are made, property accountability documents are updated and the quantity of equipment on hand is reported to all levels. Repair parts are issued to the unit (e.g., to the PLL) and are automatically reflected as on-hand. Shortages are automatically ordered and the status of orders to fill those requirements is provided routinely to the unit. All transactions are appropriately recorded in supporting financial and in-transit visibility/total asset visibility systems.

b.   **Key integrations items:**
  i.   TBD
  ii.   TBD

c.   **Key Participants:** (Organizations and Systems we must interact with to

> properly work scenario):
> i.   GCSS-Army
> ii. LMP
> iii. PLM+
> iv. DFAS
> v.   TRANSCOM

17. INTRODUCTION OF NEW EQUIPMENT INTO THE ARMY INVENTORY

a. **Definition:** Through the acquisition process a Program/Product Manager is delivering a new item into the Army inventory. The equipment is received and added to the Army's master property records. The master data and technical information would be provided by the contractor in a specified format into PLM+. Appropriate supply, maintenance and financial records at the national level would be updated. As equipment was subsequently fielded to using units their maintenance and supply/property accountability records automatically would be updated. Additionally, information would be provided as required to C2/readiness reporting systems.

b. **Key integration items:**
    i.   Technical data provided in format to allow direct entry into PLM+
    ii. IETM
    iii. REQVAL/TAADS
    iv. Automatic updating of unit and direct support level maintenance records
    v.   Automatic updating of property accountability records (property books, hand-receipts, shortage annexes/component listings)

c. **Key Participants:** (Organizations and Systems we must interact with to properly work scenario):
    i.   PM/Acquisition systems (ACE?)
    ii. PLM+
    iii. GCSS-Army
    iv. LMP

8.   Public Sector Change Management: What are the ERP Issues?

Rainer A. Sommer

INTRODUCTION

In many ways, the notion of change management invokes a certain level of mistrust among many managers who have actually participated in large-scale business process re-alignment. This is especially true when that re-alignment is based on packaged enterprise resource planning (ERP) software. Now that ERP is making inroads into public sector organizations, it is not surprising that many agencies and departments are falling victim to the same mistakes that contributed to the failure of many private sector implementations. Foremost among these mistakes is the lack of (1) a change management strategy, and (2) lack of high-level managerial oversight. In essence, by purchasing ERP software, the organization is committing to new business processes that are optimized and integrated within a pre-packaged information system. Whether packaged business processes actually make sense within the context of the organizational mandate and the underlying business model will have to be determined during the scoping phase of an implementation. In many cases, rather than develop proprietary applications, agencies are willing to give up certain specialized requirements in favor of an integrated business model that is designed into the ERP software. This trade-off between proprietary application development and off-the-self business software will determine how little or how much of a change management initiative must be fielded, and to what degree high-level managers must control the project. Given the nature of government contracting, there are many pitfalls in public sector ERP implementations which are not necessarily as critical in the private sector. This chapter will attempt to make a fair comparison between these two implementation domains.

DEFINING MANAGERIAL OVERSIGHT

In almost all cases, when management first makes it known that they are considering ERP as a way to improve organizational efficiency, the rank and file are enthusiastic and supportive because the project is considered to be an

IT solution. Most employees are in favor of these solutions for they perceive IT as a means to automate mundane and repetitive tasks. Given that ERP is generally classified as an information system, the initial project management tasks are often delegated to the IT department. In general, this is the first pitfall that high-level managers should recognize and avoid. Even though the end-result of an ERP implementation is an integrated business information system that will be managed by the IT department, the initial planning and scoping phases are strictly business management tasks and therefore the IT department (which is a staff function) should not be included in any decision(s) that affect business priorities and process design.

Why is it so important to exclude IT during these initial planning phases? Let us consider the organizational landscape. High-level managers, regardless of whether they operate in the public or private sector, have the mandate and responsibility to plan for, and set the business direction of the organization. Once they have made the decision to implement ERP, they must also take responsibility for defining the best business process architecture within the ERP system to meet the goals and objectives defined in the organizational plan. This often is very difficult to do because there is no single 'cookie cutter' method or tool that will ensure that the strategic direction set forth by management will actually be implemented within the process architecture of the ERP system. This happens because management requires useful methods and tools that can capture organizational planning information (based on managerial concepts) and then convert it into 'concepts' that are understandable by the individuals charged with actually designing and implementing the ERP system. On the other hand, there are many methodologies and tools that allow information to be linked vertically between the business process design level and the systems implementation level. These relationships are depicted in the following figure Figure 8.1.

Figure 8.1 indicates that there are many methodologies (and automated tools) that can align the process analysis phase of a project with the data modeling phase. Unfortunately, there are no clear methods or automated tools that allow managers to align the organizational planning phase of a project with the process analysis phase.

Vertical integration represents the alignment of all three phases; organizational planning, process analysis and data modeling. This is very important, for it helps one to recognize that in many instances when new business processes are aligned with redesigned information systems, the older systems often do not perform as expected. In such situations the original planning goals set out by management were not enforced or completely understood at the Business Process Re-Engineering (BPR) level and thus the supporting information system did not function as management had expected.

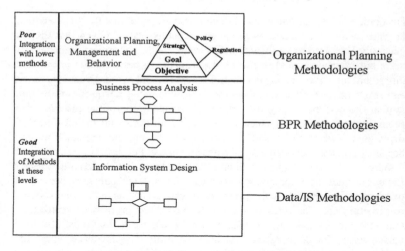

Figure 8.1: Vertically Integrated Modeling Methodologies

In the end, strategic planning is an 'art' and must be driven by management to align strategies with organizational business process initiatives. Fortunately for ERP software customers, once the strategic planning phase is completed, the vendor can provide methods and tools along with a descriptive process architecture that together show which business process functions are executed within the ERP software. With the SAP ERP software for example, the company provides a very detailed graphical process 'reference model' that shows the customer the most common business processes executed by the SAP business applications. Along with the reference model SAP provides a suite of decision support tools (Value SAP tools) that allow managers to first view and then choose the appropriate business process functionality to implement. Collectively, these activities are designed to set project 'scope'. We will look at scope issues in more detail in the latter part of this chapter. However, suffice it to say that scope is a high-level managerial function and thus must be controlled by a committed management team.

Managerial Responsibility

As shown in Figure 8.1, high-level managers are responsible for linking the strategic direction of the organization to executable business processes. Hopefully, these processes will eventually be instantiated within the ERP system. To accomplish this mission, middle management, which owns the processes, must be held accountable to high-level management for aligning the processes within the ERP system. This is where change management becomes critical. Without a sound change management plan at this juncture, many ERP projects begin to unravel.

As stated previously, most rank and file members are usually not aware of the significant managerial and process impacts of ERP implementations. Research has shown that middle management is usually supportive of ERP as long as the project is IT centric; with a perceived notion of automating 'As-Is' processes. However, once the project is underway, managers quickly begin to understand that ERP is cross-functional in nature and its design breaks traditional organizational barriers along budgetary, political and leadership lines. This realization often leads to real and/or imagined insecurities about job loss, reassignment, loss of control, status, influence and many other factors. The end result is that middle management will actively, and in many cases, subversively, work to derail the ERP implementation. To help mitigate these problems management must educate the rank and file on ERP concepts and be proactive in providing continuous feedback on project status. Many of these issues must be addressed by a change management strategy that is implemented at the beginning of the project. This will help greatly in keeping middle managers focused, motivated and committed to a successful implementation.

So what does such a strategy look like? There are many variants, but some common elements exist. A sound change management strategy should be based on the following:

- High-level managerial commitment: if the top executive members remain positive, engaged and proactive, then lower rank and file members will follow suit.
- Education: all management personnel should be educated on ERP concepts and the cross-functional implications of the implementation. Those members designated as Subject Matter Experts (SMEs) should receive specialized training to help them understand the methodologies and tools used in the scoping effort.
- Participation: high-level managers must adopt an open door policy in order to allow individual participation in the project. If someone wishes to participate, and has value to add to any phase of the implementation, they should be included. Sidelining individual initiative will only foster discontent and resistance.
- Reassurance: middle management, as well as rank and file members, must not feel that their jobs and careers are at risk. To that end, the change management plan should include high visibility provisions for a myriad of personnel and human resource issues (i.e., retraining, education, early retirement incentives, lateral career track incentives, etc.).

- Feedback: a continuous and open flow of communication about the ERP implementation project is an effective way of dealing with uncertainty. Many organizations publish project newsletters, offer seminars, invite speakers, and encourage management to develop personal relationships with rank and file members to stimulate two-way communication flows to maintain a positive level of trust between high-level managers and workers.

Although these change management factors are based on common sense ideas, the most important issue remains education. Management must educate workers on the fact that ERP-based business processes will cross organizational boundaries, be directed by new management teams and are supported by a new integrated information infrastructure. This concept is referred to as Horizontal Enterprise Integration (Figure 8.2).

In Figure 8.2, the customer order process does not contain all functions within each domain, even though the management solution spans all three domains. This presents a problem to traditional line managers. Since the new organization will be aligned cross-functionally in the ERP system, line authority will also be transferred to a new process owner. This simple horizontal re-alignment has a profound impact on the functional authority within the 'old' domains. Under this alignment, domain managers must now support the process owner. Hence their authority is moved from 'line' status to 'staff' and performance is measured on how well they support the process owner. This causes much conflict and uncertainty in traditional organizational hierarchies which have depended on autonomy and domain control to effectively compete with other domains.

Modern functional 'stovepipe' units are the result of a competitive organizational culture. In the traditional business culture it is the individual business units that must compete for, and constantly justify the resources that they expend. To meet those demands, and in order to remain competitive against other units, functional managers will put in place many artificial barriers designed to limit personal interaction and information flow between the units. The barriers can take many forms, but in order to force compliance, are mostly policy and regulatory in nature. In extreme cases, many stovepipe managers have deliberately put in place systems and applications that are not compatible with many systems and applications in competing organizational domains. These actions manifest themselves in decreased cross-functional transparency. The end result is a culture of mistrust and indifference when addressing the needs of the customer.

In addition to the regulatory and policy constraints, top-level functional managers will often put in place information system and personnel management models that are designed to keep cross-functional information flow to a minimum. System constraints are usually implemented intentionally as 'standalone' information architectures that are not compatible with those of other business units, thus creating an 'island of automation' within the corporate landscape. To further restrict cross-functional interaction many mid-level management positions are created to act as information brokers with other departments or business units. These mid-level managerial 'check-stations' exist solely for the purpose of managing the information flow dictates of top-management (Sommer, 1998) (Figure 8.3).

Horizontal Enterprise Integration

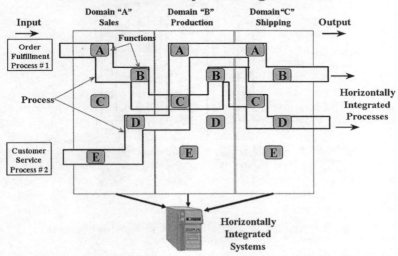

Figure 8.2: Horizontal Enterprise Integration of Processes and IS

ERP-based business systems challenge existing management structures and information systems. Because 'old' management structures and systems are usually not capable of supporting new process oriented organizations; change is inevitable, hence there are costs. One critical cost that Gulledge and Sommer (2002) identified, is that horizontal process flow eliminates 'check stations' between the boundaries of organizational domains (e.g., between Sales, Production, and Shipping) Figure 8.3.

In general, cross-functional process management has driven corporate downsizing at the check stations (i.e., the 'white collar' mid-managerial level) because organizations no longer manage by domain, but rather by horizontal process (Figure 8.2). Horizontal process management has eliminated much of the mid-level bureaucracy that was established to support standalone departments (domains), where many of the same activities had been duplicated in each domain.

Domain Oriented Organizational Structure with "Check Stations" at the Boundaries

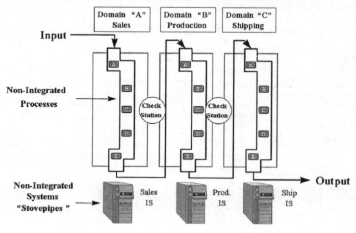

Figure 8.3: Organizational Structure with 'Check Stations' at the Boundaries

ERP systems force an organizational structure that breaks down functional stovepipes and eliminates 'islands of automation'. Within this structure many of the traditional middle management 'check stations' become unnecessary. This fact is made perfectly clear when we look at the dizzying array of middle management layoffs that occurred in the mid-to-late 1990's (Sommer, 1998). White-collar middle management positions at the staff level were being eliminated in large numbers because the functional power structures that supported these positions were eliminated by ERP. At the same time traditional line managers also felt the repercussions of an ERP-based process management model. Although the old stovepipe line management hierarchies still existed, their functional duties were now focused on supporting new cross-functional processes and the all powerful process owner. In effect it was the process owners that gained power while former, functionally-oriented middle managers were directed to support the process owners.

MIDDLE MANAGEMENT FIGHTS BACK

The commercial success, publicity and marketing of ERP systems has led many organizations to take a serious interest in reducing information technology expenditures and streamline business processes. Although many middle managers will agree with this 'cost and efficiency' premise, they become less than enthusiastic with the concept once they fully understand the repercussions of a process-oriented organizational structure. The realization that ERP software provides tight control and high visibility into all aspects of the business does not align with the traditional management concepts advocated by most mid-level management cultures. In many organizations these cultures have flourished simply because they controlled critical processes, assets, and information in an autonomous and isolated manner. Opening up the process to external scrutiny and oversight is in direct conflict with this middle management power structure. Hence, ERP becomes a concept that threatens the existence of that power structure.

To effectively deter or stall ERP implementation initiatives we find that middle management has devised four key principles that can delay, or to a certain degree 'derail' an ERP implementation.

- The 'Uniqueness' Principle: this concept suggests that for a business unit to be excluded from ERP standardization, said unit will attempt to put forth a convincing argument that their processes, products, culture are so unique that standard commercial ERP software would hamper and degrade their overall effectiveness.
- The 'Buy-in but don't Commit' Principle: this concept suggests that a business unit will have representatives on most ERP decision making committees. The mandate for the representatives is to gather enough strategic information to justify and support the traditional stovepipe business unit structure to higher management while at the same time providing ambiguous support to the company position on ERP. To a lesser extent a secondary mandate involves the spreading of ambiguous, and in certain instances, misleading information to the ERP decision making committee in order to disrupt/prolong the decision making process.
- The 'Focus on the Data' Principle: this concept is intended to re-focus vital business process issues by injecting a requirements mandate that is strictly data driven. By re-baselining requirements from process to data, the door is open to very low-level interoperability, data interface, and application integration issues. This low level approach can effectively stall and, in many cases, conflict with the higher-level ERP business process scoping effort. Once the data driven requirements concept is in place it will take a

very long time for upper management to refocus the various committees on a business process-oriented approach.

- The 'Don't Made a Decision until the Last Minute' Principle: this concept is intended to delay any decision making progress to a point where the pressure of time, or upper-level managerial mandates will force action from middle managers. However, by following such an unstructured and reactive decision making path enough confusion and ambiguity can be interjected in the ERP deployment strategy that many of the problems/issues will have to be revisited and revised at a later date. This effectively stalls the ERP effort and introduces increased cost, frustration and confusion.

GENERAL PUBLIC SECTOR CONSIDERATIONS

In some ways many of the afore-mentioned ERP implementation issues are very generic. However, there are several unique differences between public and private sector organizations that can greatly influence the implementation of an ERP system, and are directly affected by the unique cultures that dominate these domains.

Foremost, the private sector is governed by competitive advantage and profit. Bearing in mind that most all private sector process change efforts are driven by customer satisfaction and profit, organizations are streamlining operations by:

- Flattening organizational structures,
- Managing across organizational boundaries (cross-functional process management),
- Eliminating redundant 'check stations', and
- Outsourcing non-core activities.

These cultures are most often 'shocked' into change by a committed top-level management team that understands and embraces competitive advantage and customer centric service models. They understand the risks associated with ERP and are willing to do whatever it takes to break the traditional functional hierarchy and implement a process-centric management model. They also realize that if the implementation is successful, information flow and transparency will greatly enhance productivity without maintaining a cumbersome legacy data processing environment.

On the other hand, public sector organizations are much more difficult to define and subsequently change. The difficulty lies in the political complexity of modern bureaucratic structures. Unlike the private sector, public sector organizations are not autocratic in nature. In the private sector, the CEO has the ultimate power. They can mandate change by manipulating budgets, and make personnel decisions (i.e., hire, fire, promote, reassign, etc.) in order to get the managerial vision implemented.

Public sector organizations manage in a much more federated style, so that no one person has absolute power to effect change. Although this model validates the 'checks and balances' of power that are necessary in any governmental bureaucracy, it does present a problem when management tries to effect large-scale, proactive organizational change. There are many commonalties with the private sector, (i.e., hierarchical organizational structures, failed BPR efforts, non-value added check stations, etc.) however, these commonalities are overshadowed by significant disjoints which fly in the face of private sector change methods. Consider the following.

- The Bottom Line: public sector organizations have no strict bottom line incentives such as profit, customer satisfaction, or competitive advantage which drive the private sector. Although the taxpayer is defined as the ultimate customer, in many instances it is almost impossible to define who the 'true' customer is because there is no clear 'payment for services' model that can be base lined in order to measure performance.
- Power Brokers: the public sector has no long-term power-brokers (such as private sector CEOs, CTOs, etc.) that can force a vision, or expend political capital to achieve a vision. Most career bureaucrats (i.e., Senior Executive Service) never have enough political clout in their position to ensure that their vision is driven to a successful conclusion. They still manage in the stovepipe model and compete for resources with other stovepipes.
- Political Appointee Constraints: most all political appointees have a very short time frame within which to drive an agenda. Realistically they must drive their initiatives during their first two years in office, because their tenure is tied to the fortunes of the presidential election. To that end they often use the last two years of their appointment to do political work, or to develop a plan for transitioning back to the private sector.
- Mandatory Rotation: within the military ranks, flag level officers (Generals, Admirals) are most often on mandatory rotations, and although they may have an ambitious agenda, they must work diligently to get even a fraction of their programs funded and completed before they are assigned to a new position. Chances are that when a new flag officer is assigned to a recently vacated position, he will only provide complete support for his own agenda and interests.

- Organizational Rivalries: to secure congressional funding, public sector organizations are forced into very aggressive and competitive rivalries. Although some of these rivalries base their roots on historical and cultural contexts, most are driven by competition for scarce resources. Nowhere is this more evident than within the US Department of Defense where inter- and intra-service rivalries are entrenched more deeply than in the private sector.
- Mid-Management Apprehension: mid-level managers can stall or 'buck' initiatives far longer than their private sector counterparts. Given the constraints associated with organizational rivalries and executive rotation and tenure, public sector rank and file can move very slowly in implementing a top-level mandate with the hope that when the leadership goes away, the mandate will also disappear.
- Innovation: in the public sector, innovative ('out-of-the-box') thinking is risky and not encouraged or rewarded. In fact most bureaucrats shun risk taking of any kind. On the 'upside', there are very few incentives for pushing an innovative agenda, while there are many disincentives for failure. Hence few managers are willing to challenge the status quo.
- Decision Making: all decisions (even at high SECDEF/Flag/SES levels) are made by committee where the prime goal is to achieve consensus. Again, much of this behavior is driven by a culture steeped in 'checks and balances'. However, the committee-based decision model has shown to be very slow in driving critical decision making, providing clear guidance, containing special interests, and garnering support from lower level managers.

These constraints are significant and greatly hamper public sector ERP-based change efforts. Most can be overcome with proper planning and a well defined change management effort. However, there is one single issue that differentiates public sector change efforts from the private sector model. When looking at public sector business change within the context of an ERP implementation, one single issue stands out: budget visibility.

The fact is that once public sector managers realize the cross-functional process change implications of ERP, they begin to understand that budget visibility and budget efficiency drive this management model. This flies in the face of public sector financial practices that have traditionally tried to hide budgetary information within overly complex process and policy architectures that support functional stovepipes. This is not to imply that public sector financial and program managers are corrupt or inept, but rather that the culture, the budget allocation structure, and the performance measurement practices of public sector organizations necessitate these actions so as to ensure that funding is at least maintained at current levels. The fear within public sector budgeting circles is that if budgets and expenditures are scrutinized over the long term, traditional and long-standing contracting and acquisition practices will come under intense scrutiny and eventually may be deemed questionable in nature and thus eliminated. This could severely curtail the organizations flexibility in managing its procurement cycles, contractor base, and general program management activities.

LESSONS LEARNED FROM PUBLIC SECTOR ERP EFFORTS

A Look at Project Scope

In looking at ERP in a public sector context, it becomes evident that there are many benefits to implementing packaged business software. However, to drive an ERP effort to a successful conclusion, the first critical step is the issue of implementation 'scope'. Scope must be loosely defined as a high-level management activity designed to identify critical business processes that must be configured in the fielded ERP system. This activity is of utmost importance, for it bounds the implementation to a set of achievable milestones within the eventual project plan. Given the critical nature of this activity, one would expect that scope definition would be considered a function to be executed by top management.

In stark contrast to the private sector, many public sector managers shun this process because it requires a documented commitment by management to take a position on radical new ERP-based cross-functional processes and practices that may not be popular with the rank and file and may not fit the culture or the political agenda of the organization as a whole. As mentioned previously, innovative thinking is not rewarded in the pubic sector; hence no bureaucrat wants to put his career on the line for an ERP implementation. So who defines scope in large public sector ERP implementations? In many cases no one.

Tragically, there are many large-scale public sector ERP projects that are either already fielded, or are in the realization phase, that do not have any formal scope definition. That is to say, no one on the management team has taken responsibility for bounding the implementation from an organizational design as well as process integration and systems interfacing perspective. Even though these systems may already be fielded, they are essentially 'flying blind' as to whether or not they are adding value to customer and organizational needs. In many cases, the ERP system is nothing more than an expensive replacement for the old legacy system. In effect, the new system adds no value except for the fact that it can execute the old process much faster. In their most basic form, these ERP systems are just processing the 'old garbage' at a faster pace.

Many argue that by not defining detailed scope, public sector managers are keeping the ERP requirements fluid, and thus more adaptable to change. This argument makes little sense when faced with the reality of ERP-based process implementation choices. By minimizing the scoping function of the ERP project, organizational, process and systems requirements start to grow disproportionately ('scope creep'). In so doing, critical processes can never be aligned to the organizational structure and the data requirements in a definitive manner. Hence the eventual configuration and testing of the integrated system will be sub-optimal.

There is also another, more politically expedient way that public sector managers can avoid taking responsibility for scope definition: Let the contractor do it. This model is actually based on a very pervasive trend in the public sector managerial mindset, namely that managers are only concerned with 'Program Management' activities and are abdicating day-to-day project management to government contractors. This model is often realized on ERP projects, where it is not uncommon for contractors to not only define scope, but also support government program managers in the project's resource allocation, subcontracting, and procurement activities. Many have likened this model to 'the fox managing the hen house', yet due to government downsizing, the contractor base in most public sector organizations has grown substantially and their responsibilities often overlap with those of their government client.

In general, there is nothing wrong with this model, when looked upon in the context of a traditional program management effort; such as a weapon system or a command and control system project. These programs have been sub-managed by responsible contractors for decades. However, ERP implementations are radically different. Here we are not developing a weapons system, but are undertaking a radical redesign of the organization as a whole. When management decides to implement ERP, they are actually purchasing a new organizational structure supported by new business processes. This affects the entire value chain of the organization, and is often of crucial importance to the federal agency system as a whole. Hence, effective contractor oversight through ERP program and project management must be of the highest priority to public sector managers. They must know what functionality is being implemented in the system, and to what extent it meets the requirements set forth in the scope document.

This latter point is of critical importance. Unless program and project managers hold their primary implementation contractor to account on meeting expected scope, there is a high probability that when problems arise (and they occur on any project) the contractor will immediately want to de-scope the project in order to stay on schedule. This trend is endemic and is a reflection of modern contracting practices within the public sector as a whole. In general, most large-scale ERP projects have been awarded under a 'fixed price' contract model. The reasoning from the government side is that once a Request for Proposal (RFP) has been priced by the contractor and subsequently competed and awarded, the government client will get a properly executed contract through which compliance and performance can be measured using traditional program management techniques. Although this line of thought makes sense from a traditional program management point of view, ERP projects are far too complex to be managed along these lines. The organizational, process, and master data requirements that are defined in the scope document, are often not clearly understood by managers; hence they must rely on their prime contractor for clarification. When the project is on schedule the contractor will provide clarification within the spirit of the contract. However, it is also often the case that when the project becomes constrained for any reason (i.e., schedule, personnel, etc.) the contractor will look for ways to redefine scope so schedule requirements are met. In many cases the scope may be redefined in subtle ways within the ERP configuration so as not to alert the customer as to significant changes. Many times this is accomplished in benign fashion by curtailing the information presented in reports and system I/O functions. On the other hand it is not uncommon for the contractor to radically de-scope entire business processes, curtail mandated legacy and support system interfaces, or eliminate critical enhanced software systems from the project entirely (i.e., customized user requirements, application software 'bolt-ons' such as document management or product management). Unless the public sector management team is proactive in understanding the ERP implementation scope and in managing its contractor base, the de-scoping can be hidden for months. It is not uncommon for contractors to hide limited, de-scoped functionality during critical milestone reviews under the guise of claiming a dependency on a future interface requirement, a specific legacy system data call, or another software vendor's functionality. Unless the program management team is intimately familiar with the implications of these issues with regard to the original scope document, they may sign a critical milestone review document and thereby release the contractor of any further responsibility.

This scenario is not uncommon; in fact it is standard practice in many federal sector consulting firms. The culture of these firms is defined by billable hours and in getting a system online as quickly as possible. A common term used by the vendor and contractor community is to 'slam the system home' and worry about fine tuning at a later date. When translated, this terminology means that the contractor is willing to sacrifice scope in order to get a system running, and that he or she will re-scope once the follow-on contract has been signed. As a result, the public sector program manager realizes too late that his original scope was sacrificed in favor of 'fixed price' contract constraints that were driven by his contractor team.

The crux of the problem lies in the fact that complex ERP contracts may only be let via a fixed price model if (and only if) the program management team can fully understand the scope of the project and then aggressively manage the contractor base.

CONCLUSION

Although many would argue the point, a properly managed ERP implementation forces positive change, and is well suited for changing the 'old' culture and traditional norms of public sector organizations. Once adequate oversight has been established, the ERP project can be used as an effective change agent. In retrospect, ERP is accomplishing what traditional BPR failed to do in previous decades. In many of the early BPR projects, agencies spent billions on re-engineering their business processes only to find out later that the cost of aligning those new processes with appropriate information technology was far too expensive. Hence, during the 1980s and early 1990s much process re-engineering was completed, but very few of those elegant processes were actually realized in cost-effective application architectures.

ERP is the antithesis of BPR because the organizational and process structures have already been pre-defined within the software. What's required from an implementation perspective is discipline in choosing which processes to implement and what organizational structure must be supported by the process architecture. Although relatively simple in concept, ERP-based process architectures are highly diverse. In many cases, the software will support many similar processes which may, or may not be appropriate for a particular organization. For instance, the SAP reference model provides for a multitude of purchase order (PO) execution scenarios. No one private or public sector organization may need to process a PO in all these variants. It is in the scope definition phase that high-level managers, supported by subject matter experts (SMEs) from the contractor as well as the agency base, must make the critical choices as to which PO processing option meets the organizational need. Once the scope has been defined, high-level managers have effectively re-engineered their company and by virtue of the ERP software, have defined a supporting application architecture within which the processes can be automated. This provides for a quick implementation cycle that effectively eliminates traditional 'analysis paralysis', and proactively forces compliance from lower-level managerial hold-outs intent on maintaining the status quo.

In lieu of the problems associated with satisfying the concerns of middle management in the ERP planning activity, many organizations are rethinking the importance of the change management function. To meet that need, all ERP software vendors include change management as a part of their implementation methodology in order to address system transition, user interface, help desk, and training issues – just to name a few. However the methodologies fall short in addressing traditional 'people issues' such as:

- Job security,
- Workplace reorganization, and
- Policy and regulatory changes that occur as a result of ERP adoption.

To address these issues well in advance, high-level organizational management must put in place a policy that provides an 'open-book' mandate to the change management team to address all critical 'people issues' (such as job security, organizational restructuring, etc.) with a very high priority. The reason behind this strategy is relatively simple: High-level management must convince the rank and file that ERP is not going to be used as an excuse to lay-off, re-assign, or eliminate jobs and/or work centers. If this effort is successful, general ERP planning and the traditional change management functions (i.e., user interface, help desk, and training issues) may be much easier to coordinate since the work force will understand and support the intent of ERP.

BIBLIOGRAPHY

Gulledge, T. and R. Sommer (2002) 'Business Process Management: Public Sector Implications', Business Process Management Journal, Vol. 8, No. 4, p. 364-76.

Gulledge, T., R. Sommer, and M. Tarimcilar (1999), 'Cross-Functional Process Integration and the Integrated Data Environment', In Elzinga, J., et al (Eds.), Business Process Engineering: Advancing the State of the Art., Kluwer Academic Publishers, Boston.

Sommer, Rainer, A. (1998) Embedding Organizational Planning Information in a Process: A Function Oriented Process Planning Approach, Unpublished Ph.D. Thesis, George Mason University, Fairfax, VA.

Sommer, Rainer, A. (2003) Business Process Flexibility: A Driver for Out*sourcing*, Journal of Industrial Management & Data Systems, Vol. 103, No.3, p. 177-83, April Issue.

PART III

RESEARCH VIEW

9. A Recurring Improvisational Change Management Methodology in Public Sector Enterprise Resource Planning Implementation

Cheryl A. Darlington

INTRODUCTION

An Enterprise Resource Planning (ERP) system is a comprehensive COTS package software solution that seeks to integrate the complete range of business processes and functions in order to present a holistic view of the business from a single information and IT architecture (Gibson et al., 1999). However, to successfully implement an ERP solution within an enterprise, there is growing evidence that failure to adopt a change management strategy leads to projects that are over budget and late. This chapter will look at the topic of organizational change management from a public sector ERP implementation perspective. It will demonstrate that a change management methodology improves success when introducing ERP within the federal, state, and local/municipal markets. The author proposes the use of the recurring improvisational change methodology to manage the change in the implementation of an ERP system. The recurring improvisational change methodology is an extension of the improvisational model proposed by Orlikowski and Hoffman (1997) and was later proposed by Sieber and Nah (1999). It employs a diagrammatic technique to outline the recurring levels of anticipated, emergent, and opportunity-based changes that arise in the implementation of enterprise-wide systems.

Information technology-related changes in public and private organizations have always been a central issue to researchers. Managing such change has become increasingly important with rapidly emerging social, economical and technological conditions. As ERP systems are becoming increasing widespread, such technologies are often seen as enabling complex changes (Nandhakumar et al., 2003). ERP software within the public sector automates business operations such as managing finances, human resources and payrolls which enables the organization to automate and streamline internal business processes. According to a report released in August 2004 by INPUT, a leading provider of government market intelligence, the federal market for ERP products and services will hit US\$7.7 billion in FY2009, a 37 percent increase over FY2004 spending of US$5.6 billion. The healthy market for ERP is attributed to the President's Management Agenda and its five areas of focus – workforce management, competitive sourcing, improved financial performance, expanded e-government and budget and performance integration. Citizens are demanding increased levels of customer service through e-government, which drives the need for real-time, interoperable and integrated systems. ERP systems provide e-government and Internet-enabled collaboration and service to citizens within the federal state and local/municipal ERP market.

Since ERP systems explicitly link strategy, organization structure, business processes and IT systems together in a coherent framework, the importance of managing change is hardly surprising. Al-Mashari and Zairi (2000) assert that effective implementation of ERP requires establishing five core competencies, among which is the use of change management strategies to promote the infusion of ERP in the workplace. Appleton (1997) claims that about half of ERP projects fail to achieve hoped-for benefits because managers significantly underestimate the efforts involved in managing change.

Organizations are highly specialized systems. In fact, they are 'coalitions of shifting interest groups that develop goals by negotiations; the structure of the coalition, its activities and its outcomes are strongly influenced by environmental factors' (Scott, 1987). Since an ERP system transforms the organization into a much more tightly coupled system, its implementation can therefore be construed as a change in the nature of the organization's life, since it suddenly precludes the existence of diverging views (Besson and Rowe, 2001). From this perspective, deployment of an ERP system can be considered as a radical organizational innovation (Besson and Rowe, 2001) and the effective management of changes caused by this innovation minimizes possible opposition of the new ERP environment.

This chapter will look at the topic of public sector change management from an ERP implementation perspective using the Sieber and Nah (1999) recurring improvisational change methodology. The recurring improvisational change methodology is an extension of the improvisational model proposed by Orlikowski and Hoffman (1997). It employs a diagrammatic technique to outline the recurring levels of anticipated, emergent, and opportunity-based changes that arise in the implementation of enterprise-wide systems. Selecting the improvisational methodology out of the traditional model is motivated by recognition that the implementation of an ERP package within an enterprise introduces turbulent, flexible, and uncertain organizational situations. Many researchers criticize that the traditional perspective of change, in which change is treated as a sequential series of predefined steps, which are bounded within a specific period of time, is becoming less appropriate in the current turbulent, flexible and uncertain environment. The unprecedented, open-ended, and context-specific nature of ERP software makes it difficult to predefine the exact changes to be realized and to predict their likely organizational impact. Rather than predefining each step to be taken and then controlling events to fit the plan, the improvisational model, defined by Orlikowski and Hoffman, recognizes that change is typically an ongoing process made up of opportunities and challenges which are not necessarily predictable from the start. Due to an ERP implementation's potential to generate several kinds of changes, the author suggests that a reoccurring improvisational model may enable organizations to take advantage of the anticipated, emergent, and opportunity-based changes that accompany the implementation of an ERP software package within the public sector environment.

ORGANIZATIONAL CHANGE IN ERP IMPLEMENTATION

The massive organizational changes involved in ERP implementation result from the shift in a business design from a fragmented, function-based organizational structure to a process-based one served by an integrated system (Davenport, 1998). Change management is particularly important in the public sector because organizations carry the burden of public expectation since the public are direct stakeholders. Success must be demonstrated and measured to provide greater accountability and more demonstrable benefits. As a result, change management plays a vital role in driving out the benefits of e-government projects such as ERP implementation.

Unlike the traditional software development approach, which promotes building systems from scratch, ERP packages encapsulate reusable best business processes and software. Enterprises purchase the package then configure their business processes and software systems to meet their requirements (Krumbholz and Maiden, 2001). Although the processes embedded in an ERP system may be customized through configuration tables, modifying a package's software code to satisfy organizational idiosyncrasies is highly impractical. This is due to the high cost of customization and upgrades, and it is is usually necessary for an organization to redefine its business processes to fit the best practices inherent in the software. As such, the changes in business processes have to be complemented with organizational changes in structure and management systems (Pawlowski et al., 1999), which must be planned strategically and implemented thoroughly (Bingi et al., 1999). Thus, ERP is often considered to be a unique kind of technological change, one that is capable of significantly transforming organizations (Boudreau and Robey, 1999) because whole departments must be retrained, jobs redefined, and procedures discarded or rebuilt from scratch (Deutsch, 1997).

The change both impacts on the organizational culture (i.e. the ways that things are done in the organization) and is constrained by it (Krumbholz and Maiden, 2001). The absence of an adequate organizational change management methodology and attitude can easily result in a total failure of the entire ERP initiative (Bancroft et al., 1998), regardless of how competent the organization is technically. Evidence has shown that organizational change has to be managed prior to, during, and after ERP implementation (Cooke and Peterson, 1998) because the implementation of ERP systems is complex, organizationally disruptive, and resource intensive change management (Volkoff, 1999).

In the article, 'Global trends in Managing Change', Lisa Kudray and Brian Kleiner (1997) offer this definition:

> Change Management is defined as the continuous process of aligning an organization with its marketplace – and doing it more responsively and effectively than its competitors. For an organization to be aligned, the key management levers strategy, operations, culture, and reward must be synchronized continuously. Since change is inevitable in ongoing process, these management levers must continuously be altered also.

In today's modern organizations, the ability to manage change successfully has become a competitive necessity. Change management refers to the effort it takes to manage people through the emotional ups and downs that inevitably occur when an organization is undergoing massive change. The meaning of managing change refers to the making of changes in a planned and managed or systematic fashion. The aim is to more effectively implement new methods and systems in an ongoing organization.

In order to prepare for the management of change within an organization, it is important to identify the forces that provoke an enterprise to change towards implementing an ERP package and the reasons why change management is difficult to accomplish.

The Need for Change

Much of the literature on change seems to assume that organizational change is triggered by a deliberate initiative by managers in response to exploit opportunities and to improve performance (Nandhakumar et al., 2003). External and internal forces to the organization stimulate change towards adoption of an ERP system. Organizations seeking to evolve to a different level in their life cycle such as going from a highly reactive, entrepreneurial organization to more stable and planned development are attracted to ERP. ERP systems are seen as optimization and integration tools of business processes across the supply chain, within and beyond organizational boundaries, implemented through modern information management systems (Stefanou, 1999). ERP is a packaged business software system that enables an agency to manage the efficient and effective use of resources (materials, human resources, finance, etc.) by providing a total, integrated solution for the organization's information processing needs (Nah et al., 2001). It is for this reason that its benefits such as improving information quality, reducing costs through retooling common business functions, and improving responsiveness and time-to-market lure organizations to change and implement ERP (Al-Mashari, 2003).

Another reason that public sector organizations are attracted to ERP is because it implies fundamental organizational changes. ERP, usually instigates, or is instigated by, business process re-engineering (Bancroft et al., 1998). The business processes embedded in an ERP package represent best practices, from which adopting organizations can benefit. Benefits include streamlined business processes, better integration among business units, and greater access to real-time information by organizational members. For many organizations, the implementation of an ERP system has the potential to provide dramatic gains in productivity and speed (Davenport, 1998).

Why Change Management is Difficult to Accomplish
Organizational-wide change is difficult to accomplish because there are strong resistances to change. Resistance is a force that slows or stops movement and is a natural and expected part of change, but progress without resistance is impossible (Maurer, 1996). People are afraid of the unknown and many people do not understand the need for change. Many are inherently cynical about change, particularly from the many ERP implementation failures described in the press today. Many doubt there are effective means and reasons for implementing an ERP system because such a change may go against how employees believe the business should be run. Another reason for apprehension and resistance is the change in roles and responsibilities due to the change in the ERP enterprise architecture. Many users may raise issues about their computer illiteracy, and their current successful fulfillment of their job duties without the help from an ERP system. Other users may believe that their jobs will be threatened by the new system, or that they are uncertain about how to do their job within the scope of an ERP system. Yet another group of employees may stress values such as the importance of existing power and authority structures, which may be jeopardized by the new ERP system.

There are many sources and types of user resistance to a new technology implementation, such as ERP. According to Sheth (1981) there are two fundamental sources of resistance to innovations like an ERP system;

perceived risk and habit. Perceived risk refers to one's perception of the risk associated with the decision to adopt the innovation. Habit refers to current practices that one is routinely doing. However, there are many enabling factors that will contribute to reducing employee's resistance to ERP implementation.

Enabling Conditions

Certain aspects of ERP and the implementing organization must exist to enable the efficient adoption of an improvisational change model. Literature research suggests that an important influence on the effectiveness of any change process is the interdependent relationship among organizational, technical and people dimensions. The difficulties many organizations have had with change management depend in large part on an inadequate recognition of interdependencies among technology, practice, and strategy (Brynjolfsson and Hitt, 1996). Milgrom and Roberts (1988) show mathematically how interactions can sometimes make it impossible to successfully implement a new, complex system in a decentralized, uncoordinated fashion. The interrelationships between the technology, the people, and the organizational contexts (including culture, structure, roles, and responsibilities) are enabling conditions that are critical to success.

Executive Commitment and Leadership
Since change is almost always resisted, all change requires the support of key executives and sponsors. Their job is to prioritize and decide what changes will happen, ensure resources are available and lead the change effort. It is also their task to assess the positive and negative impacts of the change and actively motivate and encourage the change process. This signals the importance of the change throughout the organization and facilitates the congruence between the overall ERP vision and the change process.

Within the public sector, the organizational structure is complex, consisting of many departments and divisions, each having their own manager, business rules, and processes. Depending on the structure and depth of the implementing organization, sponsors may need to exist at many different levels in the organization. However, most major change initiatives will fail without an executive level senior sponsor. Defining the role of the sponsor at different levels in the organization provides leadership by example, overcomes managerial resistance, and creates an open culture of well-understood objectives and goals.

Understood Imperative
Undertaking major change is a difficult and often painful process for most organizations, regardless of whether the ERP implementation is in response to a current problem or a new opportunity. Organizations that manage the ERP implementation effectively tend to be driven to make the change by an urgent and powerful force, either the cost of leaving a problem unresolved or the cost of missing the opportunity. If the cost of either is not sufficient, the chances are the change initiative will be overtaken by more important events. It is also imperative that the execution teams develop an appealing vision of the future and identify and quantify the objectives and drivers of the business imperative. Once the ERP objectives are clearly defined, transformational, charismatic, and visionary leaders can then communicate it to the whole organization. If the entire organization understand clearly the objectives of the ERP implementation and how the changes can be beneficial for them, they will be willing to emotionally support the changes and willing to give their best to ensure the smoothness of the overall process (Susanto, 2003).

Unless the imperative is well understood by everyone, the change initiative may not succeed because people adopt a change more readily when they have 'bought into' it. When 'buy-in' is an after thought or a weak effort at best, the outcome of the change initiative can be disappointing.

Team Working and Environment
To have any chance of success employees affected by the change need to be a part of the ERP implementation. Users and employees need to be involved in the decision-making process rather than being forced to accommodate and accept the implementation. There are a number of techniques to involve different levels in the organization, particularly those outside the main project team that are described in many different journals and trade magazines. Engagement is built through the communication of the overall objectives and imperatives as well as project progress, through soliciting their input to the design of the new process, by listening to their concerns and providing reassurance right from the start of the project and by proving the knowledge and understanding they will need to put the change into operation.

New Skills and Knowledge
Introducing ERP change invariably means that staff will need to acquire new competencies, skills, and knowledge. This may involve changing working methods and processes they have developed and redefined over many years. As performance usually decreases until new skills are established, training is an integral part of ERP implementation. Enterprises should consider tailoring courses for in-house delivery, and using the practical 'learning by doing' approach in their courses.

Governance Support Structure and Organizational Clarity
Changing the way business is delivered often imposes change on the structure of an organization. Governance in general means the controlling and reporting structure for a project. The objective of governance is to establish an overarching communication and control model whereby executive leadership can establish the proper levels of ownership over operations and ensure that all policies and procedures are properly enacted. Within the public sector, the political composition of many government agencies can change frequently, affecting the leadership and objectives of the project, thus creating a challenge for ERP implementations. As such, the new organization needs to be supportive of the new processes and ways of working and accountabilities need to be aligned to responsibilities and job descriptions and procedures. Government agencies that are successful at introducing change define the new working practices first, and then define the structure and organization in a way that sustains and reinforces the changes being made. Ultimate responsibility and accountability for the project must be clearly defined and accepted at an appropriately high level within the organization to ensure change management success.

Dedicating Resources for Ongoing Support
An on-going change process requires dedicated support over time to adapt both organization and the technology to changing organization conditions, use practices, and technological capabilities. Opportunity-based change, in particular, depends on the ability of the organization to notice and recognize opportunities, issues, breakdowns, and unexpected outcomes as they arise. This requires attention on the part of appropriate individuals in the organization to track use of the technology over time and to implement or initiate organizational and/or technological adjustments, which will mitigate or take advantage of the identified problems or opportunities (Orlikowski and Hoffman, 1997).

Comprehensive Communication
Keeping the general workforce informed of what is happening, why and how it will affect them and what will be expected is essential if resistance and conflict is to be minimized and blockers neutralized. A careful balance must be struck between too much communication, which leads to 'communication fatigue', and too little, which leads to dissociation. The communication needs therefore must be regularly re-evaluated.

Organizational context is an enabler of change management. A flexible change model, while likely to be problematic in a rigid, control-oriented or bureaucratic culture, is well suited to a more informal and cooperative culture. However a commitment to total quality management, a focus on organizational learning and employee empowerment, as well as a long-term time orientation – were particularly compatible with the improvisational model used to manage ongoing organizational changes around the new software development technology (Orlikowski and Hoffman, 1997).

Traditional versus Improvisational Models

There are many different methodologies for implementing change. One approach is rather traditional and stipulates that a team begins with a plan placing considerable effort on ensuring every aspect of the project runs according to the plan (Sieber and Nah, 1999). However, when the technology being implemented is new and unprecedented, and additionally has an open-ended and customizable nature, an improvisational model providing the flexibility for organizations to adapt and learn through use becomes more appropriate (Orlikowski and Hoffman, 1997). Such is the case, the author believes, with ERP packages available today.

Traditional Model

There are many different organizational change methodologies. One simple team-based approach begins with a premise that places considerable emphasis at ensuring the effort meets the criteria set forth in a detailed plan. (Sieber and Nah, 1999). In the traditional three-stage Lewinian change model of 'unfreezing, change and refreezing', the organization prepares for change, implements the change, and then strives to regain stability and the status quo as soon as possible. Such a model treats change as an event to be managed during a specified period as a contrast to be viewed as an ongoing event (Nilsson et al., 2001). However, when we examine how change actually occurs in practice, people respond to conditions as they arise, often in an ad hoc fashion, doing whatever is necessary to implement change (Orlikowski and Hoffman, 1997).

The traditional model is appropriate for relatively stable, bounded organizations whose functionality is sufficiently fixed to allow for detailed specification. Today however, organizations implementing ERP are complex enterprises and given the more turbulent, flexible, and uncertain organizational and environmental conditions, such a model is becoming less appropriate (Orlikowski and Hoffman, 1997).

Another reason why the traditional model for change management is difficult to enact is 'evident when organizations use information technologies to attempt unprecedented and complex changes such as global integration or distributed knowledge management' (Orlikowski and Hoffman, 1997). As in ERP implementation, organizations need to redefine and integrate core corporate functions and processes that were previously managed independently. As a result, ERP implementations represent a new way of doing business that is unfamiliar and unknown since the core corporate activities are transformed. Typically, there is some understanding of the magnitude of such a change, but the depth and complexity of the interactions among these activities is only fully understood as the changes are implemented. Planning in such circumstances is more effective as an ongoing endeavor, reflecting the changing and unfolding environments with which organizations interact (Orlikowski and Hoffman, 1997).

The Improvisational Model

In ERP implementations, 'predicting the technological changes to be implemented and accurately predicting their organizational impact is not feasible' (Orlikowski and Hoffman, 1997). As a result, there must be a more appropriate way of thinking about change that reflects the unprecedented, uncertain, open-ended complex, and flexible nature of ERP software packages.

Orlikowski and Hoffman (1997) present an improvisational model for managing technological change built on the belief that executives should begin with an objective rather than a plan, and respond to conditions as they arise in an ad-hoc fashion. Based on this model, the team enacts 'an ongoing structure, responds to spontaneous departures and unexpected opportunities, and iterates and builds on each other over time' (Orlikowski and Hoffman, 1997). Efforts are directed at reaching the objective rather than following a plan. The underlying theme is that the team will do what it takes to achieve the objective (Sieber and Nah, 1999).

The improvisational change model recognizes three types of change:

(1) Anticipated changes are those that are planned ahead of time and occur as intended.
(2) Emergent changes are those that arise spontaneously from local innovation and that are not originally anticipated or intended.
(3) Opportunity-based changes are not anticipated ahead of time but are introduced purposefully and intentionally during the change process in response to an unexpected opportunity, event or breakdown.

There are two assumptions made by this model: (1) changes associated with technological implementations constitute an ongoing process rather than an event with an end point after which the organization can expect to return to a reasonably steady state, and (2) All the technological organizational changes made during the ongoing process cannot, by definition, be anticipated ahead of time (Sieber and Nah, 1999).

This improvisational model also assumes there will be road bumps along the way towards reaching the objective. The uniqueness of the model is: (1) the flexibility to transform some of the obstacles into positive emergent and opportunity-based changes that will enhance the overall effectiveness of the organization, and (2) the acknowledgement that emergent changes exist and that they have a profound effect on enterprise-wide implementations (Orlikowski and Hoffman, 1997).

It is important to note that not all ERP implementation situations require the use of an improvisational change model. It is most appropriate for open-ended, customizable technologies or for complex and unprecedented change (Orlikowski and Hoffman, 1997). Some cultures may not support learning and experimentation, and may not be receptive to the successful use of an improvisational model. However, as these organizations attempt to implement new organizational forms, they too may find an improvisational model to be a particularly valuable approach to managing technological change in the 21st Century (Orlikowski and Hoffman, 1997).

THE RECURRING IMPROVISATIONAL CHANGE METHODOLOGY

The recurring improvisational change methodology proposed by Sieber and Nah (1999), is an extension of the improvisational model originally proposed by Orlikowski and Hoffman (1997). It employs a diagrammatic technique to outline the recurring levels of anticipated, emergent, and opportunity-based changes that arise in the implementation of the enterprise-wide systems. In Sieber and Nah's article, the diagrammatic approach was illustrated in the context of an SAP implementation at the UN. In this section, the recurring improvisational change methodology will be illustrated via a desktop case study (a hypothetical research view based on data collected from publicly available data) performed in the context of Nestlé's SAP implementation in June 2000, which shows how the methodology could be applied in a large organization.

Nestlé, Desktop Case Study Description

Nestlé, with more than US$50 billion in annual revenue, over 237,000 employees, just under 500 factories in 84 countries, and over 8,000 food and beverage products sold in literally every country in the world, has committed to consolidate and standardize its business processes worldwide as part of a program to realize more than US$1.8 billion in benefits by 2006. Nestlé has extensive business operations that reach into every corner of the globe. Just under 500 factories around the world manufacture beverages, milk products, culinary products and cooking aids, chocolate and confectionery, bottled water, pet care, and pharmaceutical products. These products include Nescafe instant coffee, Perrier bottled water, breakfast cereals, Kit Kat chocolate bars, Stouffer's prepared meals, Buitoni pasta, and Maggi cooking sauces. Established since 1866 in Switzerland, Nestlé is today, the world's largest food and beverage company and is committed to an 'e-revolution' to boost revenues, slash US$3 billion from the cost base, and consolidate and standardize the business processes to reach the ultimate goal. The company's worldwide operations, which currently let each factory conduct business according to rules that fit the local business culture, are costly and inefficient. For example, Nestlé can not leverage its worldwide buying power for the raw materials used in its products, even though each factory uses the same global suppliers. This is because each facility negotiates its own deals and its own prices (Konicki, 2000). As a result, there were enormous variations in processes such as paying 29 different prices for vanilla to the same supplier, and comparisons were impossible because each facility had its own naming conventions.

Prior to 1991, Nestlé was simply a collection of independently operating brands/divisions with autonomous operations, such as Stouffer's and Carnation, owned by the Swiss-based parent. In 1991, different divisions were united and reorganized into Nestlé USA. These divisions reported to Nestlé USA instead of the parent company, though they were free to make their own business decisions. An information audit showed that Nestlé had around 140 different financial systems. The audit showed that Nestlé had a mismatch of systems, which consisted of 900 IBM AS/400 midsize computers, 15 mainframes, a variety of operating systems, including UNIX, various versions of Windows, and SAP R/3 already implemented at a handful of sites (Konicki, 2000). These systems were not integrated with headquarters and as such, data was transmitted to headquarters via Electronic Data Interface (EDI) or slow dial-up lines.

Top executives at Nestlé realized that to compete in e-commerce and leverage the business potential of the Internet, the company had to standardize its business processes and IT infrastructure. 'We are moving more and more into the area of e-business, and it is vital to offer our people the world over an efficient work environment and powerful functionality that is at the leading edge', says Peter Brabeck-Lemathe, CEO of Nestlé. Nestlé USA wanted to use economies of scale, common processes, systems and organizational structures across eight or nine autonomous divisions. Similarly, the parent company intended to standardize systems across its autonomous divisions in over 80 countries. Nestlé realized that common systems would create savings by aggregating demand and sharing data between its divisions thereby eliminating multiple purchasing systems. The objective of Nestlé's worldwide business and IT re-engineering project are to create and adapt common business practices to leverage the size of Nestlé as strength, not a liability, unite and align Nestlé on the inside in order to be more globally competitive on the outside, and unlock potential benefits by harnessing the power of e-business, with a focus on customer/channels and consumers.

To support the transformation, in June 2000, Nestlé signed a much publicized US$200 million contract with SAP for its global enterprise business transformation initiative. Nestlé proposed to centralize operations for its 230,000 employees in nearly 500 facilities (with more than 200 operating facilities) spread over 80 countries by deploying mySAP.com ERP applications and enterprise portals. An additional US$80 million would be spent on consulting, maintenance and software upgrades during the first three years of the rollout (Manage-Mentor, 2002). This was the largest software sale in SAP's history. Nestlé USA also embarked on an SAP project code-named BEST (Business Excellence through Systems Technology) in 1997.

The pact between Nestlé and SAP offers employees worldwide access to mySAP.com workplaces. Nestlé's global SAP project, which is tied into a larger US$500 million hardware and software data center rehaul, will be integrated with its US subsidiary's ERP project. The data center rehaul involves consolidating its information technology operations now based in more than 100 sites, into five international GLOBE data centers around the world. The regional data centers will be located in Sydney, Australia, Phoenix, Arizona, and Frankfurt, Germany; while two GLOBE data centers, one for the company consolidation and the other one for development, will be installed in Bussigny, Switzerland. In 2002, Nestlé announced that IBM will be the exclusive provider of servers, storage systems and database software for the next five years for the GLOBE data centers at the heart of Nestlé's comprehensive, worldwide business transformation initiative. The agreement for IBM to build technology e-infrastructure for the data centers is valued in excess of US$500 million. For the first time management at headquarters will be able to see company-wide aggregate data. For example, sales information will be used to reduce overstocking shelves and subsequent spoilage of product.

Nestlé is confident this e-business move will provide employees an effective work environment, reinforced functionality that will give them the leading edge in performance, functionality, and productivity. As the chief officers at Nestlé feel, MySAP.com workplace will help them build a robust, tightly integrated IT infrastructure permitting focused customization to user needs. Nestlé USA's Chief Information Officer, Jerri Dunn claims that to date, the six-year BEST project cost US$200 million and has saved the company US$325 million. Regardless of the project's return on investment, Nestlé learned the hard way that an enterprise rollout involves much more than simply installing software. Dunn says 'when you move to SAP, you are changing the way people work, challenging their principles, beliefs and the way they have done things for many years' (Worthen, 2002). As a result, the major software implementation is not really about the software but about change management.

Nestlé's Improvisational Change Model

Figure 9.1 represents the improvisational change model diagram for Nestlé USA's implementation of SAP. The diagram illustrates some of the changes that have occurred at Nestlé emanating from the larger anticipated change of implementing the global SAP implementation. From the diagram, one can discern the recurring changes and how one change leads to another. In general, each anticipated, emergent or opportunity-based change is expected to lead to more levels of anticipated, emergent, and/or opportunity-based change (Sieber and Nah, 1999). Due to the limited research literature available on the Nestle' SAP implementation, the author cannot discern every change caused by the implementation. As a result, the diagram only describes some of the changes that have occurred based on literature research found by the author.

From the diagram, Nestle' has realized two major anticipated changes: the formation of a common methodology for Nestlé projects worldwide and technology standards for every Nestlé Company to follow, and the data center rehaul. In 1991, Nestlé created a common methodology for their projects worldwide and common technology standards for every Nestlé Company to follow. Nestlé realized that common systems across the Nestlé empire would create savings through group buying power and facilitate data sharing between subsidiaries. The data center rehaul involved consolidating its information technology operations now based in more than 100 sites, into five international GLOBE data centers around the world.

To further illustrate the application of this methodology, the author will expand on the anticipated change of developing a common methodology and technology standards.

An emergent change that was not originally anticipated or intended was the divisions' non-compliance with the developed methodology and standards. The parent company realized that few of the streamlined methodology and technology standard recommendations had been implemented. This was despite the fact that the company could benefit from savings through group buying power and data sharing between subsidiaries.

Another anticipated change was Nestle' USA's mySAP.com role-based workplace implementation. Nestlé USA's Chairman and CEO Joe Weller coined the term 'One Nestlé' to reflect his goal of transforming the separate autonomous divisions into one highly integrated company. To realize that vision, in October 1997, the company formed a key stakeholder team of 50 top business executives and 10 senior IT professionals to create a set of uniform best practices that would become common work procedures for every Nestlé division. This business process re-organization involved streamlining all divisional functions, which included manufacturing, purchasing, accounting and sales (Worthen, 2002).

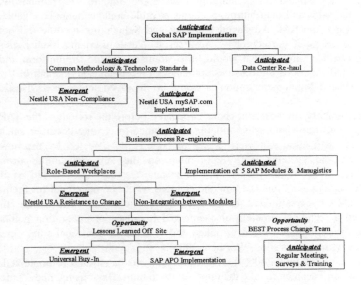

Figure 9.1: Proposed Nestle Improvisational Change Model

These streamlined functions formed the basis for the anticipated change of role-based workplaces that were designed for distinct parts of the Nestlé Organization. These workplaces will enable the individual business divisions within Nestlé to swiftly implement the streamlined functions and also adapt them to the specific needs of the individual markets. Role-based workplaces are customized, personalized, role-based portals that are the 'my' part of mySAP.com. Employees in all areas, all over the company can access both application and content on the Nestlé Intranet as well as the Internet to create an effective work environment (Webscribes, 2001). The workplaces assist in defining the role of each employee in the company, which enables employees to perform their job functions better. It empowers the worker and continuously redefines his role in within the company, resulting in enhanced work performance (Webscribes, 2001). These roles are constantly refined and configured to further adapt to the requirements of Nestlé's global workforce, through collaboration between SAP and Nestlé. The productivity of the worker is increased and the daily tasks can be completed from anywhere in the world. Workplaces help in managing external relationships, administration and maintenance. These tools also help in implementing security and safeguarding the system (Webscribes, 2001).

Nestlé anticipated implementing five SAP modules – purchasing, financials, sales and distribution, accounts payable, and accounts receivable. At the time, the SAP Advanced Planning and Scheduling module did not meet the needs of the company. As a result, Nestlé used the Manugistics supply chain module, and it would be customized around the uniform and streamlined functions and business processes (Worthen, 2002). Each of the five SAP and Manugistics modules would be deployed across every Nestlé division.

Unfortunately, an emergent change appeared before the rollout of the SAP modules and the Manugistics module. Resistance to change occurred since none of the groups that were going to be directly affected by the new processes and systems were represented on the key stakeholder team (Worthen, 2002). Employees did not understand the reasons or objectives of the ERP implementation and how the changes would be beneficial for them. Nestlé USA underestimated the need to manage the resistance to change. In addition, a technical problem also emerged because the integration points between the modules were overlooked and as a result, divisional silos were replaced with process silos (Worthen, 2002).

As a result, in June 2000, the BEST project was halted and re-organized. The company decided to take the opportunity to hold a lessons learned offsite meeting to re-evaluate the project. The outcome of this opportunity-based change resulted in a new beginning for the BEST project. Two emergent changes resulted. The Manugistics module would be replaced with the SAP Advanced Planner and Optimizer (APO) supply chain module. In addition, steps would be taken to ensure the universal support (buy-in) from key division heads so that all employees would know exactly what changes were taking place, when, why, and how (Worthen, 2002).

By April 2001, the opportunity to create a new process change team to act as a liaison between the divisions and the BEST project team emerged. The process change team anticipated that regular meetings and surveys with the division heads and employees would be needed. To assist with the transition to the new ERP system, Nestlé provided extensive one-on-one, classroom and computer-based training.

By the time that the BEST SAP implementation project was complete Nestlé employees will be able to access mySAP.com via an internal, role-based portal customized by the functions of the employees job. Even, Nestlé's trading partners and customers will be able to access the company through private and secured exchanges, expanding the business outside the company.

CONCLUSION

The implementation of an ERP software solution does not have a specific beginning and an end but rather is a continual process in which change must be managed. This chapter has demonstrated that the recurring improvisational methodology can be used to manage the anticipated, emergent and opportunity-based changes that result from an ERP implementation.

BIBLIOGRAPHY

Al-Mashari, M. 2003. A Process Change-Oriented Model for ERP Application, International Journal of Human-Computer Interaction, 16(1), 39–55.

Al-Mashari, M. and Zairi, M. 2000. Information and Business Process Equality: the Case of SAP R/3 Implementation. Electronic Journal on Information Systems in Developing Countries, Vol. 2.

Aladwani, A. 2001. Change Management Strategies for Successful ERP Implementation. Business Process Management Journal. 7(3), 266–75.

Appleton, E.L. 1997. How to Survive ERP. Datamation. 50–53

Bancroft, N.H., Seip, H. and Sprengel, A. 1998. Implementing SAP R/3: How to Introduce a Large System into a Large Organization, Greenwhich, CT: Manning.

Besson, P., and Rowe, F. 2001. ERP Project Dynamics and Enacted Dialogue: Perceived Understanding, Perceived Leeway, and the Nature of Task-Related Conflicts. The Database for Advances in information Systems. Vol.21, No.4.

Bingi, P., Sharma, M.K. and Godla, J.K. 1999. Critical Issues Affecting an ERP Implementation. Information Systems Management. 16(3), 7–14.

Boudreau, M.C., and Robey, D. 1999. Organizational Transition to Enterprise Resource Planning Systems: Theoretical Choices for Process Research. Proceedings of the Twentieth International Conference on Information Systems, 291–99.

Brynjolfsson, E., and Hitt, L. 1996. Paradox Lost? Firm Level Evidence of the Returns to Information Systems Spending. Management Science.Vol.42, No.4, p. 541–58

Brynjolfsson, E., Renshaw, A., and Van Alstyne, M. 1997. The Matrix of Change. Sloan Management Review. 37(18) p. 2-38

Cooke, D. and Peterson, W. 1998. SAP Implementation: Strategies and Results (Research Rep. No. 1217-98-RR). New York: The Conference Board.

Davenport, T.H. 1998. Putting the Enterprise into the Enterprise System. Harvard business Review 76(4), 121–31.

Deutsch, C.H. 1997. Software that can Make a Grown Company Cry. The New York Times.

Gibson, N. Holland, C.P. and Light, B. 1999. Enterprise Resource Planning: A Business Approach to Systems Development. Proceedings of the 32nd Annual Hawaii International Conference on. HICSS-321999.

Holland, C.R. and Light, B. 1999. A Critical Success Factors Model for ERP Implementation. IEEE Software, 16(3). 30–36.

Konicki, S. 2000. Nestlé Taps SAP for E-Business. Information Week. 26, June 2000. 185.

Kudray, L. and Kleiner, B. 1997. Global Trends in Managing Change. Industrial Management. 39(3). 18

Krumbholz, M. and Maiden, N. 2001. The Implementation of Enterprise Resource Planning Packages in Different Organizational and National Cultures. Elsevier Science.

Manage-Mentor. 2002. Nestlé's ERP Saga – Part I. The Manage Mentor. http://www.themanagementor.com.

Maurer, R. 1996. Beyond the Wall of Resistance. Maurer and Associates.

Milgrom, P. and Roberts, J. 1988. Communication and Inventories as Substitutes in Organizing Production. Scandinavian Journal of Economics. 90(3) 275–89.

Nah, F., Lau, J., and Kuang, J. 2001. Critical factors for Successful Implementation of Enterprise Systems. Business Process Management Journal. 7(3), 285-96

Nandhakumar, J., Rossi, M. and Talvinen, J. 2003. Proceedings of the 36th Annual Hawaii International Conference on Systems Science (HICSS–36), p. 240–49.

Nilsson, A.; Josefsson, U. and Ranerup, A. 2001. Proceedings of the 34th Annual Hawaii International Conference on.Systems Science (HICSS–34), p. 207–15

Orlikowski, W. J. and Hoffman, D. 1997. An Improvisational Model for Change Management: The Case of Groupware Technologies. Sloan Management Review. 38(2). 11–20.

Pawlowski, S. Boudreau, M.C. and Baskerville, R. 1999. Constraints and Flexibility in Enterprise Systems: A Dialectic of System and Job. Proceedings of the Fifth Americas Conference on Information Systems, 791–93.

Scott, W. 1987. Organizations: National, Natural, and Open Systems (2nd edn..), Englewood Cliffs, NJ: Prentice Hall.

Sheth, J. 1981. Psychology of Innovation Resistance, Research in Marketing, Vol.4, 273–82

Sieber, M. and Nah, F.H. 1999. A Recurring Improvisational Methodology for Change Management in ERP Implementation. Proceedings of the Americas Conference on Information Systems (AMCIS), August. pp. 797–99.

Slater, D. 1999. The Hidden Cost of Enterprise Software. CIO Magazine. 15, January.

Stefanou, C. 1999. Supply Chain Management (SCM) and Organizational Key Factors for Successful Implementation of Enterprise Resource Planning Systems. Proceedings of the Americas Conference on Information Systems. 800–02.

Susanto, L. 2003. Change Management and ERP Implementation: Side-by-side. Retrieved 5, April, 2004, from a search on Google.

Volkoff, O. 1999. Using the Structural Model of Technology to Analyze an ERP Implementation. Proceedings of the Fifth American Conference on Information Systems. 235–37.

Webscribes 2001. Nestlé: e-workplace. Retrieved from http://www.ciol.com/content/search/showarticle1.asp?artid=35517

Worthen, B. 2002. Nestlé's ERP Odyssey. CIO Magazine.

10. Transaction Costs in Public Sector Information Technology Implementations

Douglas W. Frye

INTRODUCTION

In recent years, the ongoing desire of the US government to make its operations more efficient has manifested itself in the leveraging of information technology (IT) in accomplishing its various missions. This chapter describes the goals set by the government toward improving its functions, then moves into a discussion of the similarities and differences between the public and private sector operating environments, followed by a description of how IT is able to benefit an organization through reducing transaction costs. Then, the roles of how effort levels and commitment to a project are formed are discussed through the prism of x-inefficiency and principal-agent theory. The ill-fated Federal Acquisition Computer Network is then used to illustrate how a lack of support within the government can doom a program to failure. Finally, the Balanced Scorecard as a methodology to affect effective change management in an organization is discussed.

GOVERNMENT ACKNOWLEDGMENT OF NEEDED EFFICIENCIES

In February 2002, the Office of Management and Budget (OMB) published a study detailing four areas in which the Federal Government could improve:

- Government-to-Citizen (G2C): accomplished through building easily accessed 'points of service' for citizens to complete their business quickly and with as little hassle as possible.
- Government-to-Business (G2B): accomplished through eliminating redundant data collection and providing better communication.
- Government-to-Government (G2G): make it easier for subordinate government units (state and local) to meet reporting requirements and increase the quality of collected data for performance management.

- Internal Efficiency and Effectiveness (IEE): leveraging technology to reduce costs and improve quality of administration through 'using industry best practices in areas such as supply-chain management, financial management and knowledge management.' (OMB, 2002)

This chapter focuses on the fourth item. The same report lists four phenomena that have prevented the federal government from increasing productivity in the past:

- Program Performance Value: rather than judge their IT systems based on how well they deliver services to customers, the evaluation stems from to what extent they facilitate the internal workings of the agency.
- Technology Leverage: automating existing processes was the main function of IT in the 1990s. Creating more efficient and effective solutions is now possible, based on observation of the private sector.
- Islands of Automation: mirroring the Project Directive Line Item (PDLI) accounting practice in the federal government, IT systems have been bought to address internal needs, rarely with any consideration given on their ability to interact with other systems. The result is a traditional 'smokestack' configuration in which each separate entity must specifically request needed information from other offices.
- Resistance to Change: traditional organization structures and budgeting processes have perpetuated 'obsolete' bureaucratic divisions in the federal government. Fear of restructuring has led to resistance against change, even though it would likely help the government better accomplish its goals.

It is uncontroversial to state that the public and private sectors operate under very different regulatory regimes. There are similarities, however. Starling (1998) lists the following five:

- Planning: establishing visions and goals for the future of the entity,
- Decision making: knowing the requirement, identifying alternatives and selecting one to accomplish the stated goal,
- Organizing: dividing the labor, setting schedules and grouping tasks into organizational units,
- Leading: using influence to motivate employees to meet objectives by working at a high level of commitment, and

- Controlling (implementing and evaluating): monitoring the progress of a project and altering employee activity as necessary to ensure project success.

In addition to the similarities, there are four ways in which private administration and public administration differ:

- Structure: authority to make policy and personnel decisions is diffused in public agencies relative to industry.
- Incentives: the motivation to satisfy those who provide the resources to one's livelihood is strong. Thus, even low-paid workers in private industry will be more motivated to respond to customer needs than highly-paid civil servants.
- Setting: because of the assumption of almost complete transparency in US government administration, it is much more likely that decisions made for 'business reasons' in the public sector will be challenged or stymied through what amount to public relations campaigns in the press.
- Purposes: while both the private and public sectors use inputs to produce outputs, the public sector output is much more difficult to quantify performance measures (provide for the common defense?) and compare alternative programs (should the US$10 million be spent on a weapons system or medical research?).

With these conflicting operating environments, it becomes difficult to rationalize using identical approaches to implement new programs intended to improve efficiency and save money, as irrational as that may seem at first glance. Blum and Naylor (1968) reviewed two competing methods of evaluating programmatic success. The first method, from Shubik (1958, in Blum and Naylor, 1968), is *economic man*, a person who attempts to maximize return. The second type of person from Simon (1957, in Blum and Naylor, 1968), is *satisficing man*. This person is more concerned with what is the best feasible alternative within a range of acceptable returns and tends to be more comfortable in a bureaucracy. A cursory comparison of the private and public sectors would lead one to conclude that the private sector would conform to the economic man model while the public sector would be identified with satisficing man. While it is likely true that each more closely fits the definition of the concept to which is has been assigned, it is theorized that the proposed study would discover examples of alternate behavior found in each sector (where the public sector will attempt to maximize return and the public sector will satisfice). Should the question 'Is it important for you to maximize your monetary return while minimizing cost?' be posed to public and private sector officials, the answer would assuredly be; 'yes'. The actual difference in perspectives and practice occurs in the actual program implementation.

Public officials are less likely to operate efficiently than their private sector counterparts, for three reasons:

- Government officials are less able than businesspeople to define the most efficient path to the goal. Aside from the stated programmatic goal, there are often contextual goals (equity, for example) preventing the economically pure solution from being enacted.
- Government officials are not as motivated as the private sector to generate savings. They will not personally realize the savings they generate (residual claims), and thus will not have the economic self-interest of the private sector.
- Government officials lack the same authority to implement efficient programs vis-à-vis their private sector counterparts (Wilson, 2001).

Box (1999) argues that the difficulty of trying to balance being an entrepreneur while considering the input of several interested parties on top of trying to maximize the economic efficiency of the program may have the ultimate impact of making the decision-making process of the official opaque to the public, because of the bureaucrat's ability to act without review (in the 'entrepreneurial spirit'). This lack of transparency is not in favor in the US, and would likely not be tolerated. Reich (1988) forwards a two-faceted approach, namely that there is balance to be struck between 'intermediating among interest groups' and 'maximizing net benefits.' Comparing the referees of the intermediater, who enforce fairness and non-market objectives, versus the analyst maximizer, charged with finding the best economic solution, which furthers the argument that the public servant finds him/herself in an untenable position. Finally, Bellone and Goerl (1992) forward a four-layered model: entrepreneurial autonomy versus democratic accountability; public entrepreneurial vision versus citizen participation; entrepreneurial secrecy versus democratic openness; and entrepreneurial risk taking versus democratic stewardship, to illustrate the tension between the roles of public and private managers.

Information Technology Fostering Change

In addition to helping streamline the supply chain, information technology now gives organizations the ability to integrate their front- and back-office business processes into a more 'flat' or 'seamless' ERP regime that leverages information technology's ability to distribute information to authorized parties to allow what were formerly non-directly communicative, or 'smokestack' sections of an organization to share information instantaneously. Rather than a customer-service representative being required to telephone or e-mail a colleague and force a client to wait for a response to a query, ERP solutions employ integrated applications with all information relevant to a customer 'case' available to all authorized system users. (See Figures 10.1a and 10.1b.) This real-time ability to access the most recently updated status (dependent on the recency and accuracy of the update) as well as to generate reports is, according to Ptak and Schragenheim (1999), critical to allow decision makers to make good business decisions. ERP entails all relevant functions for a client requirement, including, among other things: product design, pricing and availability, production status, shipping status and technical documentation, as well as internal information such as materials planning (ibid.).

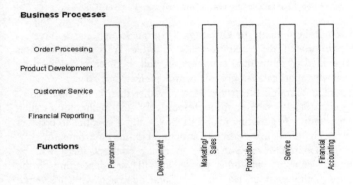

Figure 10.1a. Non-ERP Enabled Processes (Adapted from Perez et al, 1998)

The Role of Information Technology in Reducing Transaction Costs

With significant parts of the private sector now using IT to implement process-based management styles rather than simply automating existing procedures and with the public sector wishing to do so (OMB, 2002), it is relevant to discuss the benefits IT can have toward reducing transaction costs when properly implemented. To use procurement as an example, Malone and Laubacher (in Wetty and Becerra-Fernandez, 2001) argue that IT aids organizations through:

- Transacting at a Distance: rather than being required to choose from only those suppliers whose catalogs are at hand, IT makes it possible to research sources through a wider geographic and supplier 'space'.

Business Processes

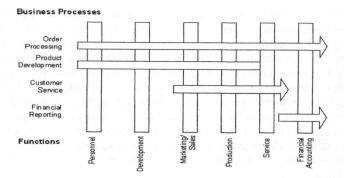

Figure 10.1b. ERP Enabled Processes (Adapted from Perez et al, 1998)

- Match Requirements to Offerings Through E-markets: a buyer is able to match their requirements to what is featured on sites maintained by individual suppliers as well as those maintained by those who aggregate supply in a common electronic space.
- Negotiate Through Electronic Means: rather than being required to negotiate face-to-face or through relatively slow technologies such as fax, online negotiating enables a buyer and a supplier to conduct their negotiations in an efficient structured online environment.
- Design Contracts via Software: in every contract there will be common elements and other parts that will vary depending on the nature of the contract. Having a modular approach with pre-vetted sections stored electronically and included when needed is an efficient use of IT, with the caveat that one must be vigilant as to when the use of a revised section rather than a template is necessary.
- Monitor Compliance with Technology: the use of IT to enable the extended enterprise allows a buying organization to verify delivery schedules, quality and other factors relevant to its requirements.

Wetty and Becerra-Fernandez (2001) contend that trust is a crucial matter in reducing transaction costs and notes that savings may be derived through each of the following generators of transaction costs: search costs, information costs, bargaining costs, decision costs, policing costs and enforcement costs. In this way, the role of individual choice in determining what to do is minimized. The optimal solution has been determined through the IT system's configuration and implementation, reducing individual discretion and the decision time associated with such discretion (Leibenstein, 1987).

A benefit of this reduction in individual discretion is that there is a lowered risk of sub-optimal or corrupt procurement practices. A government official would be prevented from awarding a contract to a relative or friend, or an audit would 'raise a red flag' as to the transaction. It would also, according to Leibenstein (ibid.,) avoid a decision maker reverting to a 'default setting', producing a suboptimal outcome. Of course, this may also disable well-intentioned contracting officials from awarding a contract to the best potential recipient, but the purpose of the public sector rules set is to prevent abuse, rather than to provide optimality. In addition, Odom (2003) argues that the facilitation of purchasing will allow procurement officials to concentrate more on managing the organization's relationship with the supplier.

Leibenstein's Discussion of Effort Levels

Nobel Prize-winning economist Harvey Leibenstein advocated the theory of 'x-inefficiency', which argues that rather than considering data at the organization level one would gain more useful insight by looking at the actions of each individual. Throughout Leibenstein's work is the idea of constraining influences. The first constraint focuses on tradition, in that 'things have never been done that way before, so it can't be the right way to do things'. The second constraint is the impact of 'horizontal' pressure (that of one's peers) on a worker. Third is the role of 'vertical' constraints, in that superiors indicate to their subordinates through their conscious and unconscious sending of 'signals' as to the effort level expected on the job (Leibenstein, 1978).

Leibenstein (1976) elaborates on the impact a superior may have on their workers in his discussion of the carte-blanche principle, which notes that when someone has the ability to impose their choice of bureaucratic constraints with impunity, the result will make people less likely to take initiative, in that the onus to overcome when trying to innovate or change standard operating procedure would make a person who would otherwise be willing to try new things unwilling to take on what would amount to two additional tasks: discovering and implementing the new way of doing things on top of convincing the bureaucracy to allow the new process to be implemented. This has important implications in the private sector, in which one may argue the number of bureaucratic hurdles to cross makes civil servants unwilling to innovate.

Inert Areas

In attempting to innovate and adapt to an ever-changing procurement environment, an organization must be able to bring in, digest and leverage information to the greatest extent possible. To wit:

> One of the firm's most important decision areas lies in recognizing signals from the environment. First the firm must distinguish between routine signals, and those which indicate changes in the environmental situation, or changes in potential technology. Second, problems may result from the evaluation and channeling of signals from those who receive them from the external world to those within the firm who can best evaluate them and make decisions on that basis. A large number of nonoptimal states persist in this area. Those who receive important signals may not be in a position to process them and send them through the appropriate channels. This is an area where a possible arbitrary use of power within the firm as well as arbitrary bureaucratic procedures may prevent or fail to motivate those who have useful information about the environment to channel such information to the appropriate decisionmakers (Leibenstein, 1976).

It is the ability to bring in, assess and process the information available that contributes to the optimization of the production process and leaves open the possibility that what Leibenstein (1978, 1987, for example) refers to as *inert areas* will result in sub-optimal production implementations. The neoclassical model assumes decisions are made on the firm level, but when humans are required to determine how to accomplish a task, such as awarding a contract, they are, while aided by information systems, forced to make a final determination using their own judgment. In doing so Leibenstein notes that people are subject to a certain level of inertia in their decision-making process (1978), and that when within the bounds of their inert area they will default to a familiar decision. A person typically settles into an inert area through discerning what are known and allowable 'effort positions', and assigns a level of utility derived from that position. When a person achieves equilibrium between effort and reward that person adopts that position as their personal optimal effort position (rarely the maximum utility position). This 'position preference' leads people to avoid looking outside their inert area because of monetary and emotional cost associated with finding a new effort position. The more entrenched this position preference the more likely attempts will be made to avoid deriving a new one (Leibenstein, 1976). The roles of calculated (maximizing) and uncalculated (non-maximizing) decisions are important.

Principals and Agents

When a person is taken outside the boundaries of their inert area they begin to look for new solutions (Leibenstein, 1987). 'In some contexts, it may be especially useful to distinguish two separate components of the inert area theory: (1) the utility cost of moving away from the present position–i.e. 'packing up' costs, so to speak and (2) the utility cost of getting set up and 'settling into' the new position' (ibid., 1978). The relationship between performance and pressure was established by Yerkes and Dodson. The Yerkes-Dodson Law notes that effectiveness increases until a certain level of stress is reached, flattens out for a time and then decreases as stress begins to overwhelm one's ability to perform under the resultant pressure (1908, in Leibenstein, 1987). The distinction between how a person with a direct financial stake (a principal) and a person who 'only works there' (an agent) determines their effort level is very important. In a typical principal-agent relationship the principal will attempt to compel agents to act in the best interests of the principals (Wright and Mukherji, 1999). Because principals are seen as having a neutral reaction to risk and agents are argued to have an aversion because of their inability to spread their interests across several jobs (Eisenhardt, 1988), principals will therefore attempt to wrest an effort level closest to maximum efficiency from their agents while the agents will use their superior knowledge to pursue goals that aid them rather than the principal (Donaldson, 1990). Leibenstein (1976) notes that in large companies and public sector-owned companies the workers are so far removed from the true principals that they often do not have a strong connection to the organization. It becomes very difficult to define 'gain' when there is a large amount of organizational distance between principals and agents. 'In some ultimate sense we attempt to interpret gain in terms of utility, but this ceases to be a clear notion when the principals are a large group of shareholders or all the citizens of a country' (ibid.).

In discussing the efforts of agents versus those of principals it is worth briefly noting two studies addressing their motivations mentioned in the same literature as x-inefficiency. Wrong (1961, in Eisenhardt, 1988) noted that factory workers tend to be more responsive to attitudes than to monetary inducements, while J.P. Shelton (in Leibenstein, 1976) found in a study of a chain of restaurants that those run by franchisees were more profitable than those run by owner-operators. An executive in the company concluded that 'franchise-owners just watch the little things closer; they utilize the cooks and waitresses better: they *reduce waste* (emphasis added in Leibenstein, 1976.)

The Federal Acquisition Computer Network (FACNET):
What Not to Do

The network, established by law in 1994, required that all federal government agencies be able to solicit competitive award contracts through FACNET by 1999. The goal of the program was never met, however, as agencies found that there were cheaper, faster and more technologically reliable ways to promulgate their procurement functions (*Government Contract Litigation Reporter*, 1997). Ultimately, the US Congress repealed the requirement to use FACNET in 1997 (Wallace, et al,. 1998). This inability to force compliance, even through congressional mandate, calls into question the staying power of any implementing agency, civilian or government, that does not have the sheer magnitude of an IBM with regard to compelling compliance with a prescribed program.

FACNET was designed to leverage electronic data interchange (EDI). After a requirement was generated, a buyer would put its requirements data into a standard form and send it to a contractor-run value added network (VAN), which would distribute the data to connected contractors. In response, contractors wishing to respond to the solicitation would send their bids to the government over the VAN. When the winning bid was selected, the government would send a notification over FACNET to the vendors. (GAO, 1997)

Actual use of the network was dominated by one agency, the US Department of Defense (DoD), which had installed EDI in 300 locations over the first two years FACNET existed, accounted for over 90 percent of transactions. In all, only approximately two percent of eligible transactions were performed using FACNET. The most damning indictment was the comment that FACNET was already obsolete when it was deployed, less effective than using the Internet to search online catalogs. Figure 10.2 illustrates the distribution of system types 17 agencies reported using. It is interesting that only about a third of agencies were using FACNET despite the federal mandate to do so.

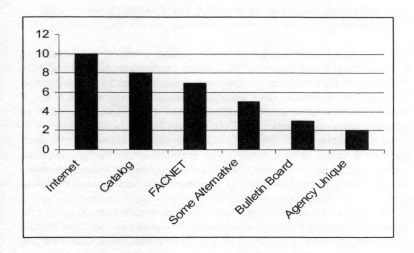

Figure 10.2. Electronic Procurement Methods (Source: GAO, 1997)

Issues Contributing to FACNET's Failure

There were several shortcomings contributing to FACNET's ultimate demise. They may be separated into two categories: technical and management. On the technical side, there were many problems reported by both purchasing agencies and vendors. 'Lost, late, and duplicate transactions and network interruptions have frustrated government and industry users and delayed procurements' (GAO, 1997). The lack of adequate infrastructure, management and vendor database was cited as significant barriers to acceptable usability (ibid..). To wit:

In April 1996, a senior contracting official at the Army's Training and Doctrine Command stated that FACNET did not function well enough to support the Command's requirements in a meaningful way. He noted that outgoing FACNET solicitations had been lost or received by vendors as late as 2 weeks after transmittal and responses vendors had sent out soon enough to be on time were received at the Command several days after the closing date. He added that (1) vendors were frustrated about spending time and money to become FACNET-capable and then discovering that their quotes did not make it through the system and (2) vendors often faxed their quotes to Training and Doctrine Command buyers, in addition to transmitting them through FACNET, to ensure receipt. Another Army contracting activity reported that its buyers routinely mail out copies of FACNET award notices because vendors complained that they were not receiving them through FACNET (ibid.).

In a notable case another Army command found that executing a procurement action through FACNET actually took more time and was more cumbersome than their manual process. From the vendor perspective, it would not make sense to incur potentially substantial setup and VAN fees if their business volume generated through FACNET would not realize an adequate return on investment (ROI) (GAO, 1997).

As of October, 1996 'DoD officials reported that only 4,000 of about 300,000 federal contractors had valid registrations in the government's central vendor registry' (Power, 1997). In the GAO report, it was noted that it was necessary to give awards to unregistered vendors because it would otherwise be impossible to meet all governmental requirements (GAO, 1997). And while some government agencies were reporting success in reducing contract lead times, competition and vendors from which to choose, the general consensus of the agencies was that it actually took more time and consumed more resources than the manual processes (ibid.).

When considering the management issues surrounding FACNET, there were several factors mentioned by government agencies which contributed to its ineffectiveness. First, noted government contractor Dendy Young (in Hulme, 1997), the decision to award a contract was based exclusively on price, ignoring other relevant factors from past performance such as quality and timeliness. This problem was far from being the most significant issue, however:

- Lack of a business case: in the conception and planning stages, no 'business case' was composed to assess the likely costs and revenues/savings from system implementation. Even if a business case is not ultimately accurate in estimating the funding and time required to successfully implement a program the process one goes through to generate a legitimate business case affords a superior perspective on what to expect than if one goes without it.
- Lack of consistent funding and staffing: during the program, there was what the GAO report referred to as 'ad hoc' funding. The funding was not certain from year to year, therefore, any multi-year plans for the system would be absolutely contingent on non-guaranteed funding. Without adequate staffing, there is a serious lack of continuity in the 'corporate knowledge' of the program, which often leads to a large body of knowledge 'walking out the door' and on to other projects.

- Lack of Leadership and Program Management: A large number of agencies interviewed for the GAO report voiced the concern at the lack of leadership and program management, attributed largely to the uncertainty of consistent funding. As a result, individual agencies were 'on their own' in formulating a FACNET implementation strategy. According to some vendors, this resulted in 'inconsistent and, in some cases, directly opposite practices' at different agencies. For example:

1. some buyers accept fax queries for more information and send faxes to clarify FACNET solicitations, while other procuring activities no longer permit use of faxes and will ignore any incoming fax messages,
2. there seems to be no consistent policy covering procurements exempted from use of FACNET, and
3. the number of days a solicitation remains open is highly variable (GAO, 1997).

Without these three elements it is very difficult at best to implement a program of any size, let alone one intended to process billions of dollars of transactions every year. Paperless contracting, especially if forced on the proposed schedule, is precisely the kind of burdensome mandate that should be avoided for exactly those reasons. Ultimately, as noted above, the requirement for FACNET compliance was removed.

The Balanced Scorecard

In the drive to present the vast amount of data available to an organization and its suppliers, a method for displaying aggregated data as it relates to organizational strategy in an easily understandable format has come into prominence in recent years and has been adopted by procuring organizations. This method, known as the 'balanced scorecard', was originally developed by Kaplan and Norton (1992) and displays an evaluation how well a supplier is succeeding in meeting their buyer's expectations for such measures as timeliness, quality, and others to be described below. But this kind of measurement 'has consequences far beyond reporting on the past. Measurement creates focus for the future and communicates important messages to all organizational units and employees' (ibid., 2001). A balanced scorecard's primary function is to link an organization's strategic goals to quantifiable measures to be shown and indicate to the reader the success or failure of the organization or its supplier to the goals (Moshonas, 2004).

In recent years, the balanced scorecard as a tool for public sector organizations has been discussed (see for example Niven, 2003). To the creators, the balanced scorecard is a key change management tool at first and then a way to monitor success in meeting the new vision of the organization's functions as defined by the scorecard. Only by being able to tie compensation and promotions to numbers appearing on a scorecard can its true utility be realized. (Kaplan and Norton, 2001a)

There are four views for a balanced scorecard (Kaplan and Norton, 2001b):

- Financial – the strategy for growth, profitability, and risk viewed from the perspective of the shareholder.
- Customer – the strategy for creating value and differentiation from the perspective of the customer.
- Internal Business Processes – the strategic priorities for various business processes that create customer and shareholder satisfaction, and
- Learning and Growth – the priorities to create a climate that supports organizational change, innovation, and growth.

In discussing the role of balanced scorecards in the public sector, Kaplan and Norton (2001b) argue that because the nature of the organizations lacks the clear 'pay for service, receive service' model it is difficult at times to delineate the ultimate customer. What the authors suggest is to have an over-arching purpose at the very top of the scorecard to define the ultimate customer. For example, in the case of the DoD, the warfighter is the ultimate customer in most cases (ibid.). A balanced scorecard for each section of an organization demonstrates to each worker how their function 'rolls up' to the next higher level and eventually how it contributes to the ultimate objective (Gumbus and Lyons, 2002.) Figure 10.3 shows visually the procession of information up and down the strategy map.

Typical Measures for Public Sector Organizations

Niven (2003) discusses various measures for public sector organizations from each of the four perspectives. From the customer perspective, such factors as the total time a system is available to users, the amount of time saved through using the new system versus the old process and the efficiency with which a system function may be completed and customer satisfaction with the system play a significant role in determining a system's success. From the internal processes perspective, a major measure to take into consideration is the quality of the product or service delivered. For a repair part, as an example, what is the number of defects per thousand units? The timeliness with which the products or services are delivered is also important. For employee learning and growth, the amount of training delivered to system operators is an important if rather broad measure. Looking at an 'operator error' measure would give a more realistic indication of total learning and could allow for needed retraining. Of critical importance is employee satisfaction in using the system. Turnover is caused by any of several factors, one of which is certainly frustration resulting from using a user-unfriendly computer forty hours each week. Finally, financial measures include the cost of the system per transaction or per a specific time period (week, month) and the accuracy of the data fed into accounting systems one's organization is obligated to report to. Niven (ibid.) describes the characteristics each measure should possess before it is included in a balanced scorecard:

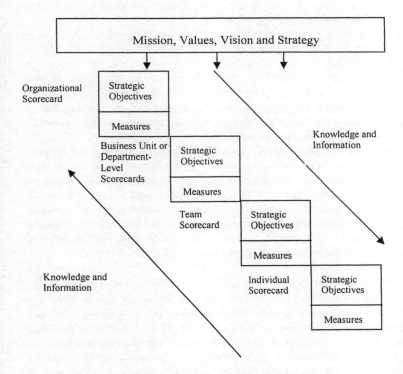

Figure 10.3: Knowledge Flowing in a Cascading Balanced Scorecard
(adapted from: Niven, 2003)

- Linked to strategy – there should be a clear link in an organization's 'strategy map' between a measure and each higher measure until eventually connecting with the ultimate strategic goal.

- Easy to understand – each measure should be defined in a way that all competent employees will understand what the measure is and what is expected of them to meet the assigned level.
- Link in a chain of cause and effect – each measure should be applicable in all four views of the scorecard, as the views are not distinct but rather one of four 'filters' to view information through.
- Updated frequently – data gathered in real time may be used to update scorecards automatically. Not updating scorecards frequently enough can result in ineffective decision-making.
- Accessible – it is important to ensure that the type of data needed to truly tell if a system is succeeding is capturable.
- Average-cautious – unusually high or low data points may result in an unrealistic viewpoint of the actual situation.
- Resistant to specific dates – Niven argues that a measure to complete a project by a certain date is more of an initiative and not appropriate for inclusion on a balanced scorecard.
- Quantitative – yes/no responses, for example, are not quantitative measures. The percentage of reports received on time, however, would be considered quantitative.
- Disfunctional – Niven uses an example of a 'wasted food' measure that actually hurt a restaurant. To avoid waste, the cooks were ordered to not prepare any food until actually ordered by patrons beginning one hour before the kitchen closed. This led to longer wait times for food to be served and resulted in lost business, overwhelming the savings realized from reduced waste. An organization should take care to ensure their well-intentioned improvement does not result in an overall negative impact.

CONCLUSION

Using information technology as a tool for increased functionality and efficiency in the government is well established. This chapter has dealt with organizational change from the perspective of the individual as to how they make and act on decisions about their effort level and how they will facilitate or, in the case of FACNET, resist changes imposed on them from above. A tool to define and communicate change and how it affects an organization is the balanced scorecard. With its current popularity, public policy officials charged with implementing programs changing an organization's processes should take the time to understand it and how it would bring itself to bear in their agency.

BIBLIOGRAPHY

Bellone, Carl J. and George Frederick Goerl; 'Reconciling Public Entrepreneurship and Democracy'; Public Administration Review; Vol. 52, No. 2; March/April, 1992; pp. 130–134.

Blum, Milton C. and James C. Naylor; *Industrial Psychology: It's Theoretical and Social Foundations*; Harper and Row; New York, NY; 1968.

Box, Richard C.; 'Running Government Like a Business: Implications for Public Administration Theory and Practice'; American Review of Public Administration; Vol. 29, No. 1; March, 1999; pp. 19–43.

Donaldson, L.; 'The Ethereal Hand: Organizational Economics and Management Theory'; Academy of Management Review; Rev. 15, No. 3; 1990; pp. 369–81.

Eisenhardt, K.M.; 'Agency and Institutional Theory Explanations: The Case of Retail Sales Compensation'; Academy of Management Journal; 1988; Vol. 31, No. 2; pp. 488–511.

General Accounting Office (GAO); Acquisition Reform: Obstacles to Implementing the Federal Acquisition Computer Network; January, 1997; Government Printing Office; Washington, DC.

Government Contract Litigation Reporter; 'FACNET Not Yet All it Was Hoped to Be, GAO Says'; 17 April, 1997; Accessed from the Factiva online database 5 December, 2003.

Gumbus, Andra and Bridget Lyons; 'The Balanced Scorecard at Philips Electronic: It's Used to Align Company Vision, Focus Employees on How They Fit Into the Big Picture, and Educate Them on What Drives the Business'; Strategic Finance; November, 2002; Vol. 84, No. 5; p. 45; accessed from the Business Index ASAP online database 19 January, 2004.

Hulme, George; 'Electronic Procurement Becomes Capitol Idea: Federal Government Using Electronic Commerce Instead of EDI'; Computer Reseller News; 11 August, 1997; n. 749; p. 100.

Kaplan, Robert S. and David P. Norton; 'The Balanced Scorecard—Measures That Drive Performance'; Harvard Business Review; January—February 1992; pp. 71–9.

Kaplan, Robert S. and David P. Norton (2001a); 'Leading Change With the Balanced Scorecard'; Financial Executive; September, 2001; Vol. 17, No. 6; p. 64; retrieved from the Business Index ASAP online database 19 January, 2004.

Kaplan, Robert S. and David P. Norton (2001b); 'Transforming the Balanced Scorecard from Performance Measurement to Strategic Management: Part I'; Accounting Horizons; March, 2001; Vol. 15, No. 1; p. 97; Retrieved from the Business Index ASAP online database 18 January, 2004.

Leibenstein, Harvey; 'Allocative Effeciency vs 'X-Efficiency'', American Economic Review, 56, 1966, pp. 392—415 in *The Collected Essays of Harvey Leibenstein: Volume 2. X-Efficiency and Micro-Micro Theory*; Kenneth Button, ed.; New York, NY; 1989.

Leibenstein, Harvey; 'Aspects of the X-efficiency Theory of the Firm'; Bell Journal of Economics, 6; 1975; pp.580-606 in Button, Kenneth, ed.; *The Collected Essays of Harvey Leibenstein: Volume 2. X-Efficiency and Micro-Micro Theory*; New York, NY; 1989.

Leibenstein, Harvey; *Beyond Economic Man: A New Foundation for Microeconomics*; Harvard University Press; Cambridge, MA; 1976.

Leibenstein, Harvey; *General X-Efficiency Theory and Economic Development*; Oxford University Press; London, UK; 1978.

Leibenstein, Harvey; *Inside the Firm: The Inefficiencies of Hierarchy*; Harvard University Press; Cambridge, MA; 1987.

Leibenstein, Harvey; 'Organizational of Frictional Equilibria, X-Efficiency, and the Rate of Innovation'; Quarterly Journal of Economics, 83; 1969; pp. 600–623; in Button, Kenneth, ed.; *The Collected Essays of Harvey Leibenstein: Volume 2. X-Efficiency and Micro-Micro Theory*; New York, NY; 1989.

Leibenstein, Harvey; 'X-Efficiency Theory, Productivity and Growth', in Herbert Giersch (ed.), *Towards an Explanation of Economic Growth*; (J.C.B. Mohr; tubingen), 1981; pp. 187–212.

Moshonas, James; 'Balanced Scorecards Lessons Learned, Part 1'; downloaded from http://www.bettermanagement.com/library/browse.aspx?mode=library&bus inesstopic=Balanced%20Scorecard, 21 January, 2004.

Niven, Paul R.; Balanced Scorecard Step-by-Step for Government and Not-For-Profit Agencies; John Wiley & Sons; Hoboken, NJ; 2003.

Odom, Steve; 'Status Report From the Trenches'; 2003; http://www.isourceonline.com/article.asp?article_id=2276, accessed 21 February, 2003.

Office of Management and Budget (OMB); Simplified Delivery of Services to Citizens; Government Printing Office; Washington, DC; 27 February, 2002.

Perez, Mario, et al; *SAP R/3 on the Internet*; Addison-Wesley; Harlow, England; 1999.

Power, Kevin; 'Agencies Opt Out of FACNET'; 10 February, 1997; downloaded from http://www.gcn.com/archives/gcn/1997/February10/govb.htm, 4, August 2003.

Ptak, Carol A. and Eli Schragenheim (Ed.); *ERP Tools, Techniques and Applications for Integrating the Supply Chain*; 1999; St. Lucie Press; Delray Beach, FL.

Reich, Robert B.; The Power of Public Ideas; Ballinger Publishing Company; Cambridge; 1988.

Schauer, F.; Playing By the Rules; Oxford University Press; Oxford, UK; 1991.

Shubik, M.; 'Studies and Theories of Decision-Making'; Administrative Science Quarterly; 1958; No. 3; p. 289—306.

Simon, H.A.; *Models of Man: Social and Rational*; Wiley; New York, NY; 1957.

Starling, Grover; *Managing in the Public Sector*; Fifth Edition; 1998; Harcourt Brace and Company; Fort Worth; TX.

Wallace, David A., et al.; 'Contract Law Developments of 1997—The Year in Review'; Army Lawyer; January, 1998; Lexis-Nexis; Retrieved 9 January, 2002.

Wetty, Bill and Irma Becerra-Fernandez; 'Managing Trust and Commitment in Collaborative Supply Chain Relationships; Communications of the ACM; June, 2001; Vol. 44, No. 6; p. 67.

Wilson, Tim; 'E-Procurement Revisited: More Than Cheap Supplies'; www.internetweek.com; 20 April, 2001.

Wright, Peter and Ananda Mukherji; 'Inside the Firm: Socioeconomic Versus Agency Perspectives on Firm Competiveness'; The Journal of Socioeconomics; May, 1999; Vol. 28, No. 3; p. 295.

Wrong, D.; 'The Oversocialized Concept of Man in Modern Sociology'; American Economic Review; Rev. 26, No. 2; 1961; pp. 183–93.

Yerkes, R.M. and J.D. Dodson; 'The Relation of Strength of Stimulus to Rapidity of Habit Formation'; Journal of Comparative Neurology and Psychology, (18), 1908, pp.459–82.

11. Testing Cultural Barriers to Enterprise System Implementations: Change Management through Organizational Culture Assessment

Mary A. Leary

INTRODUCTION

The Need to Assess Cultural Complexity in ERP Implementations

Enterprise Resource Planning (ERP) system implementation is affected by the culture of an organization and the national heritage of its employees (Huang and Palvia, 2001; Davenport, 1998) A literature search reveals that these dual elements of culture often arise when scholars discuss change management and best practices in ERP implementations. Aladwani (2001) notes the existence of three different ERP implementation strategies – organizational, technical, people. Since enterprise system implementation is grounded in changing and integrating business processes across an organization (Davenport, 1998) these people and organizational issues become quite complex when multiple cultures are involved. In addition, there is potential for cultural differences between the chosen ERP vendor and the implementation team – both the customer and systems integrator. A key element of ERP system success is rooted in understanding the issues of culture (Krumbholz and Maiden, 2001).

Some of the challenges in developing a model for the impact of culture on ERP are the convergence of so many different disciplines, disciplines that often do not integrate in the literature. Culture is a social issue, studied extensively by anthropologists. Often, political scientists and economists reference its impact. From an information systems theory perspective, culture usually arises within the context of business process re-engineering change management issues. Corporate cultural measurements usually relate to human resources employee attitude surveys. Major tools exist today that assess culture from an international attitudinal perspective, such as the World Values Survey of the University of Michigan. Delving down into each of these areas to develop a framework for measuring the effect of culture on

ERP implementation involves integrating all of these areas – sociological, anthropological, economic, psychological, managerial and technological.

However challenging, understanding the potential impact of cultural factors holds great value as a pre-planning strategy in ERP implementation. This chapter proposes an impact study on the major elements of culture affecting ERP implementation for an organization. This impact study is designed as a pre-planning tool for senior leadership as they strive to assess the cultural efficacy for an ERP project. Key journal articles in the field are discussed to derive a list of independent variables to the dependent variable of organizational culture affect on ERP implementation. A cultural effects matrix is developed with the major elements found from the literature review. The chapter's methodological recommendation builds upon past studies on the impact of cultural on ERP success.

BACKGROUND – KEY CONCEPTS AND ELEMENTS ASSOCIATED WITH CULTURE AND ENTERPRISE RESOURCE PLANNING IMPLEMENTATION

Culture

What is culture? One dictionary definition of culture is 'the behavior patterns, arts, beliefs, institutions and all other products of human work and thought, especially as expressed in a particular community or period' (American Heritage Dictionary, 2001, p. 213). Hofstede defines culture as 'collective programming of the mind; it manifests itself not only in values, but also in more superficial ways: in symbols, heroes, and rituals' (Hofstede, 2001, p. 1). Geert Hofstede did one of the most comprehensive early studies in culture. Hofstede measured international IBM employee attitudes across 72 countries with a total of 116,000 questionnaires received in two rounds – one in 1968 and one in 1972. Though national culture was the main area of interest, he also studied organizational culture characteristics. An innovative study on the cultural effects of ERP system implementation used his five dimensions: power distance, uncertainty avoidance, individualism, masculinity, and long-term versus short-term orientation (Krumbholz and Maiden, 2001). An integrative definition of culture recognizes that people's minds are patterned differently based on their national heritage and their association with certain groups or organization. These patterns manifest themselves in various ways of thinking and acting.

Organizational Culture

Evaluating organizational culture is a standard human resources practice in many companies. Large corporations often study their employees' attitudes by measuring the results of longitudinal surveys. The premise is that this provides leadership a tool to evaluate their organization and develop areas for education and intervention. Assessing organizational culture enables the implementation of required cultural change (Roberts and Rollins, 1998). Organizational culture can 'enhance or hamper organizational effectiveness' (Roberts and Rollins, 1998, p. 1). One methodology for measuring culture, Targeted Culture Modeling, suggests the existence of four work culture models with key attributes in each; see Table 11.1:

Functional *Reliability and* *Consistency*	Process *Customers and* *Quality*	Time-Based *Speed and* *Flexibility*	Network *Ventures and* *Alliances*
Being highly organized	Maximizing customer satisfaction	Decreasing cycle times	Building strategic alliances
Using proven methods and services in existing markets	Demonstrating understanding of customer's viewpoint	Develop new products and services	Developing new Products and services
Maintain clear lines of authority and accountability	Delivering reliability on commitments to customers	Maintain a high sense of urgency	Establishing new ventures and new lines of business
Limited downside risks	Improving continuously	Seizing windows of opportunity	Seizing windows of opportunity
Minimizing unpredictability	Gaining customer confidence	Adapting quickly	Using outside resources

Table 11.1: The Four Work Culture Models-Key Attributes by Rollins and Roberts

These four work culture elements influence any organizational effort that affects the way the organization does business. Corporate cultural hurdles are one reason why many ERP systems fail (Vogt, 2002), so understanding the attitudes of employees and the organizational culture is an important area of exploration.

ERP implementations change the way a company does business. The way a company conducts business also affects organizational factors. As an example, customer relationship management ERP modules change the way customer linkages occur with employees (Chen, 2001). When asked which issues most impact ERP success, CIO's rated change management and culture as two of seven success factors: 'An organizational culture where employees share common values and goals and are receptive to change is most likely to succeed in ERP implementation' (Nah and Zuckweiler, 2003). Al-Mashari and Zairi (2000) developed a diagram for what they considered the essential elements of ERP (especially, in this case, SAP's R/3; Figure 11.1)

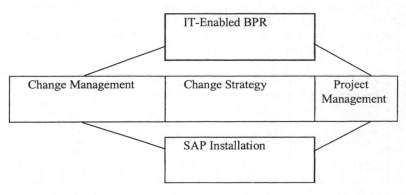

Figure 11.1: Essential Competencies for Effective SAP R/3 Implementation (Al-Mashari and Zairi, 2000)

These essential competencies are inter-connected elements, all influencing each other in implementation effectiveness. In this regard, Al-Mashari and Zairi mirror the findings of other ERP researchers. Thus, many ERP scholars recognize the importance of change management and culture as critical success factors (Nah and Lee-Shang Lau, 2001). Organizational factors such as choice and coalition-building affect the success of re-engineering business processes (Koch, 2001). Because ERP systems change the way employees work, 'early and constant' communication is critical to ease them through the transformation (Gale, 2002, p. 1). So, the communication styles of a company – whether they are open or closed – impact on ERP success. Management styles and business strategy affect multi-site ERP implementations (Markus et al., 2000). ERP planning should evaluate organizational culture issues such as communication, openness to change, teamwork, shared values, management styles and both function and process orientations.

Gunson and de Blasis deconstruct multinational organization issues influencing ERP into three areas, the organization, the individual and the workplace and recommend the exploration of nine avenues to enhance the success of ERP implementations:

- An awareness of need to balance stability and change.
- What accompanies change?
- Awareness that ERP is not just an IT project.
- A radical approach to teamwork and definition/creation of knowledge workers.
- Switching from functional to process orientation.
- Need to educate all stakeholders.
- Enterprise as change agent.
- Promote key words such as supple, evolve, survive.
- Promote fun and success.

Janz and Licker (1986) developed a corporate culture tool based on the dimensions of power, rules and values. Using a 24-question survey instrument, their factor analysis resulted in three factors: concern, contact and control. All of these concepts support the conclusions drawn from the earlier noted research. But, organizational culture, embedded in its people, is also influenced by the national heritage of an organization. Multi-national organizations face barriers when trying to standardize business systems within the diverse cultural framework of their employee population. Thus, it is important to understand the national heritage elements of culture.

National Heritage Elements of Culture and ERP

European country differences in ERP penetration rates are revealed using Hofstede's dimensions of cultural characteristics (van Everdingen et al., 2000). Sweden, Denmark and The Netherlands had 45 percent ERP penetration rates in 1998 versus the UK and Spain with 20 percent penetration rates. To explain these differences, the researchers noted the variations in uncertainty avoidance, level of individualism, power distance and level of masculinity. There were also differences, based on country of origin, in ERP selection criteria. Italian and Swedish companies rated user-friendliness high, while Spanish companies rated flexibility highly. Important selection criteria for The Netherlands were the total cost of implementation (van Everdingen et al., 2000).

Asian companies differ in their ERP implementation methodologies from their Western counterparts (Davison, 2002; Soh et al., 2000). Soh and colleagues summarized their findings by suggesting that: 'the misfit issue may be worse in Asia because the business models underlying most ERP packages reflect European or US industry practices. Procedures in Asian organization are likely to be different, having evolved in different cultural, economic and regulatory contexts' (Soh et. al. 2000, p. 2). Davison (2002) notes that cultural preferences and differences exist in: access to information, the meanings of words and numbers and re-engineering and empowerment. Many of these cultural differences relate to the earlier organizational elements. Davison also uses Hofstede's power distance variable to contrast Asian and Western authority and decision making. Asian clerical employees, according to Davison, are hesitant to accept empowerment, preferring to be told what to do because responsibility and accountability are associated with status – something that one is born into in Asian societies. Huang and Palvia found that ERP implementation factors consist of five variables across two categories, national/environmental and organizational/internal (Huang and Palvia, 2001). The five variables are economy/economic growth, infrastructure, IT maturity, computer culture and business size. An example of the role of computer culture is in India and China, where both cultures do not regard computers as 'a persuasive way of doing business' (Huang and Palvia, 2001, p. 5). In further ERP studies in India, Tarafdar and Roy (2003) developed a detailed planning system for Indian ERP implementations that appreciates the cultural and social contexts indigenous to India. His system demonstrates how ERP adoption in India closely correlates with the planning process and the management implications of each principal aspect of the planning stage. In this process, there are four aspects of the principal planning stage that the scholars feel warrant an examination of the management implications, so they go into a detailed description of each aspect along with the management implications. The four aspects and the top aspects of the management implications are noted below in Table 11.2:

Planning Aspect	Example of Management Implication
Drawing up a business case for ERP	Clear idea of the deliverables
Understanding characteristics of business and organization	Study idea of the deliverables
Assessing the IT readiness of the organization	Training and technical skill acquisition plan is required
Project Planning	Selecting modules to be implemented in each phase

Table 11.2: Four Aspects and Top Aspects of Management Implications

An interesting point with this approach is that it could be used for any country's ERP implementation. It seems possible to develop a framework that integrates organizational culture and national heritage culture as both have elements that can affect the other. Thus, when designing a testing methodology for the potential effect of culture on ERP implementations, a number of organizational attributes and attitudes will reveal total cultural enablers and inhibitors. Attitudinal variances based on value differences are illustrated by these Asian and Western countries' ERP success comparisons.

Findings – A Model for Assessing Cultural Issues in ERP Implementations

Out of the myriad of articles discussing critical success factors, ERP planning, cultural attributes of different countries, organizational cultural attributes and cultural attitudes of various stakeholders, only one article found suggests a comprehensive empirical approach to measuring ERP implementation cultural issues. The article builds on the previously noted concepts. Just as articles on ERP failure referenced culture, this study begins by suggesting there are three 'culture-related clash' points and is the only article found that mentions supplier culture versus customer culture. The researchers, Marina Krumbholz and Neil Maiden, apply Hofstede's concepts and those of another culture theorist, Trompenaars. The three clashes these researchers discuss are: (1) different national and organizational culture ERP implementation problems; (2) elements of culture, defined by their theory, are associated with problems in ERP implementation in different ways; (3) a supplier's culture can clash with the customer's culture (Krumbholz, Maiden, 2001, p. 186). By adding Trompenaars' elements of universalism versus particularism, neutral versus emotional, individualism versus collectivism, specific versus diffuse, achievement versus ascription, attitudes to time and attitudes to the environment, the researchers are able to integrate many of the concepts that are critical to ERP including communication, authority, levels of control, issues of power and individual versus organizational issues (Krumbholz and Maiden, 2001, p. 189).

There are four major hypotheses of Krumbholz and Maidens' integration of systems theory, social theory and management theory. First, they maintain that there is an integration of organizational and national culture concepts including shared values, norms and beliefs. Second, they believe that their theories help distinguish between the levels of manifestation of these factors – deep or shallow. Third, organizational culture factors are more observable while national culture sits deeper in a country's value system. Finally, overlapping facets can describe the multiple dimensions of both elements of culture. The result is an exhaustive and seemingly complete model of ERP implementation cultural issues developed into a flow chart of events, objects, goals, social interaction/reaction, customs, rituals, norms, symbols, observation, pre-conditions, post-conditions, scenarios, responsibility, heroes, agents, beliefs and values (Ibid. p. 191). To test their theory, the researchers developed a questionnaire for employees of a multinational corporation in the UK and Sweden that was implementing SAP R/3. They also used the layers of the 'culture circle', often referenced in policy journals. The circle has concentric layers moving outward beginning with norms/values/beliefs and moving through customs/rituals, heroes/myths, roles/responsibilities, symbols, style and problems, goals and actions as the last outside circle. To measure each major element of the ERP implementation, the researchers drew diagrams that showed the relationships and concepts for each facet moving from norm to value to belief to reactions/action with agent and observation relationships (Ibid. p. 198).

Using their diagrammatic instrument throughout the survey, the authors were able to identify surface problems, underlying problems and the cultural values impacting those problems. Despite the comprehensive nature of their tool, the researchers could not prove their three points regarding the effect of national and organizational culture. But, their integration of the many aspects of this ERP business problem – sociological, system, managerial, technical, and methodological – provides a ready framework to build upon for additional ERP culture implementation studies.

Though comprehensive, the Krumbholz and Maiden framework is complex. Several other ERP scholars' modeling perspectives are helpful in designing a next step study. Marietta L. Baba uses three views – people, organization and culture – and the concept of forces for and against change. Each view is analyzed for its potential as an ERP implementation risk factor in association with its level of change resistance (Baba, 2003). Action interventions are suggested based on the results of the risk assessment. A US Army ERP implementation was used as a case study for this approach. Though not integrative of all culture issues, its focus on change reinforces the crucial aspect of this critical success factor in ERP implementations.

The third set of scholars with an interesting approach for modeling ERP implementation issues is Seddon, Staples, Patnayakuni and Bowtell. With an approach that also involves multiple views, they articulate dimensions of systems success for overall IT system effectiveness. Their views are independent observer, individual, group, management/owners and country. Each element of IS systems are measured for each view. Some IS system elements are aspect of IT design, single IT application, type of IT and IT function (Seddon et al., 1999). These researchers categorize success factors of IT systems from different researchers across this matrix. What is interesting in their concept of IT effectiveness is the applicability to ERP implementation effectiveness and cultural issues.

Discussion – Designing a Study to Test Cultural Barriers and Enablers of ERP Implementation

The impact of national and organizational culture on ERP, stakeholder level of change resistance and IT effectiveness, when combined, provide an opportunity for testing culture and ERP implementation in an organization. At its base, the study of culture and ERP implementation surround the attitudes, work styles and competencies of major internal and external stakeholders – individuals, groups and organizations. Attitudes are most important in how they relate to change – especially business process changes engendered by ERP implementation – as well as tolerance of risk and ambiguity, orientation toward individual or collective good and authority. Work styles relate to decision-making preferences (consensus and participative versus autocratic and authoritarian), centralization versus decentralization, level of teamwork, level of informal networks and short-term versus long-term orientations. Competencies relate to level of communication skills, leadership skills, business acumen (as it relates to this organization's business processes), technical skills associated with ERP, level of tactical details in strategic plans, and integration of information technology and business strategic plans.

The key variables to date in organizational and national culture can be collapsed into 17 scales in these three major categories: attitudes, work styles and competencies. In some cases, competencies are not cultural, but culture will influence some skills, thus this should be in a culture assessment. This tool is not meant to test against all key critical success factors but is intended to provide an easy tool for executives to evaluate their organization's cultural readiness to undertake and succeed at an ERP project. Each of the major stakeholder groups would be assessed within these 17 scales. Total mean scores across all scales and stakeholders – internal and external – could be computed – thereby accounting for ERP supplier and systems integrator views. Descriptive statistics, factor analysis and regression might be applied to the results. A survey would be devised to score, on a 1–10 scale, the level of each of the 17 scales from highest to lowest, 1 being lowest, 10 being the highest. The 17 scales represent the top independent variables, see Table 11.3. For each question, a follow-on question would ask, is your answer related to a norm, value or belief? Negative scores would accrue for any answers that were based on any of these three elements, as they represent levels of intractability with beliefs being the deepest area.

Scales	Attitudes
1	level of resistance to change
2	toward uncertainty and risk
3	toward power and authority
4	individual versus collective good orientation
Scales	**Work Styles**
5	Consensual versus authoritarian decision-making
6	Centralization versus decentralization
7	Short-term versus long-term orientation
8	Level of teamwork
9	Function versus process perspectives
10	Level of informal networks
Scales	**Competencies**
11	leadership
12	knowledge of ERP
13	communication
14	business acumen
15	technical ERP
16	level of tactical detail in strategic planning
17	Integration of IT and business strategic plans

Table 11.3: Major Elements of ERP Organizational Readiness Cultural Assessment

If an individual or group is influenced by a norm, that represents an opportunity to create change while values and beliefs change very little over time, so focus will need to be on actions or in some cases, plan changes to keep these values and beliefs protected. As an example, if an ERP implementation is being done in an Asian country, chances are high that a focus toward empowering workers to take on greater levels of responsibility will be very difficult to achieve given the values associated with authority and status. In such cases, re-engineered business processes must take into account the need for discrete role articulation and job specificity. However, a norm that relates to a manual process versus an automated process, if discussed within the context of 'team betterness'", would probably be easily changed.

The suggested hypothesis for this study is: the cultural effects on ERP implementations are related to the attitudes, work styles and competencies of internal and external stakeholders. The dependent variable is the affect of stakeholders' culture on ERP implementation. There are two major types of stakeholders, internal and external and each type has three different views – individual, group and organization. The independent variables are the 17 scales in the three overarching categories, and a summary sheet or ERP cultural effects matrix scorecard is proposed in Table 11.4:

Attitudes:	**Work Styles:**	**Competencies:**
1) Level of resistance to change	5) Consensus versus authoritarian decision making	11) Leadership
2) View of uncertainty and risk	6) Centralization versus decentralization	12) Knowledge of ERP
3) View of power and authority	7) Level of teamwork	13) Communication skills
4) Individual versus collective good orientation	8) Short-term versus long-term orientation	14) Business acumen
	9) Function versus process perspective	15) Technical ERP
	10) Level of informal networks	16) Level of tactical detail to strategic planning
		17) Integration of IT and business strategic plans

Culture Element Scales:
score each 1-10 w/1 lowest and 10 highest score

Influences:
Internal/External Norms (-5), Values (-10), Beliefs (-20)

Table 11.4: ERP Cultural Effects Matrix Scorecard

Each of the scales would be compiled by survey responses, so a next step for this study is to design questions for each scale. Valuable source material exists in some of the aforementioned studies in crafting these questions. The cultural effects matrix could be piloted with a number of organizations and greater than 150 is recommended to ensure the results meet quantitative technique validity criteria. The benefit of having 17 scales is that this is a small enough number to provide for intervention strategies, where needed, but large enough to incorporate thought leadership to date in this area of ERP implementation cultural effects.

The expected result of this test could be a path diagram for each view with regression coefficients that show the weight and relationship of the 17 independent variables, as correlations and relationships are established, arrows would be input between each variable, example see Figure 11.2:

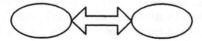

Figure 11.2: Path Model

Each circle represents one of the 17 scales. Figure 11.3 is the overall structure of the path model. Directional arrows would be added as relationships are derived from a particular organizational study.

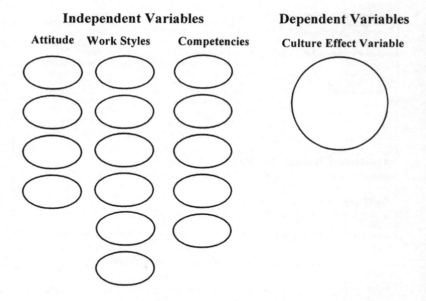

Figure 11.3: Overall Structure of Path Model

CONCLUSION AND POTENTIAL LIMITATIONS

As Hofstede cautions, any study of culture has the potential of researcher bias, so care must be taken in the evaluation of the study results. Aspects of cultural relativism and ethno-centrism are two areas for vigilance. In addition, the number of views and scales may seem quantitatively daunting and this study requires the support of a research team to help design the integration of all elements of analysis for any organization interested in applying the process. Identified norms, values and beliefs are critical to understanding the potential for intervention in the planning phase. But, despite these areas of caution, it is hoped that this recommended set of variables and process furthers the understanding of culture in ERP implementations and provides leaders of potential ERP implementations tools to assess their readiness and develop intervention strategies where cultural barriers are found. Far too many ERP implementations face failure or large cost overruns when unanticipated barriers arise, indeed, culture can be just such a barrier to change.

BIBLIOGRAPHY

Aladwani, A.M. (2001). 'Change management strategies for successful ERP implementation'. Business Process Management Journal 7(3): 266.

Al-Mashari, Majed and Zairi Mohamed. (2000). 'The Effective Application of SAP R/3: A Proposed Model of Best Practice'. Logistics Information Management. 13(3). 156–66.

American Heritage Dictionary (2001). Dell Publishing, New York. Baba, Marietta L. (2003) 'Managing Human, Organizational and Cultural Factors in LMP Implementation: Findings and Recommendations'. Prepared for: US Army Logistics Modernization Program. 9, June 2003.

Chen, I. J. (2001). 'Planning for ERP systems: Analysis and future trend'. Business Process Management Journal 7(5): 374.

Davenport, Thomas H. (1998). 'Putting the Enterprise into the Enterprise System'.Harvard Business Review. 76(4). July–August 1998. 121–132.

Davison, Robert. (2002). 'Technical Opinion: Cultural Complications of ERP'. Communications of the ACM. 45(7). July 2002. 109–11.

Esteves, Jose and Pastor, Joan. (2001). 'Enterprise Resource Planning Systems Research: An Annotated Bibliography'. Communications of the Association for Information Systems. 9(8). August 2001.

Gale, Sarah Fister (2002). 'For ERP Success, Create a Culture Change'. Workforce. September 2002. 81(9). 88–92.

Gunson, John and de Blasis, Jean-Paul (2002) 'Implementing ERP in Multinational Companies: Their Effects on the Organization and Individuals at Work'. retrieved 12/2003 from http://hec.info.unige.ch/recherches_publications/cahiers/2002/2002.07. March 2002.

Hofstede, Geert (2001). 'Culture's Consequences, Comparing Values, Behaviors, Institutions, and Organizations Across Nations'. Sage Publications.

Huang, Z. and P. Palvia (2001). 'ERP implementation issues in advanced and developing countries'. Business Process Management Journal 7(3): 276.

Janz, Tom and Licker, Paul (1986). 'Transforming a Measure of Corporate Culture To the Information Systems Area: The IS Review'. Association of Computing Machinery online database.

Koch, Christian (2001). 'BPR and ERP: Realising a Vision of Process with IT'. Business Process Management Journal. Bradford. 7(3). 258–66.

Krumbholz, Marina and Maiden, Neil (2001). 'The Implementation of Enterprise Resource Planning Packages in Different Organizational and National Cultures'. Information Systems 26. 185–204.

Markus, M. Lynne, Tanis, Cornelis, and Fenema, Paul C. (2000). 'Multisite ERP Implementations'. Association for Computing Machinery. Communications of the ACM. 43(4) April 2000.

Nah, Fiona Fui-Hoon and Lee-Shang Lau, Janet. (2001). 'Critical Factors for Successful Implementation of Enterprise Systems'. Business Process Management Journal. 7(3). 285–96.

Nah, Fiona Fui-Hoon, Zuckweiler, Kathryn M. (2003). 'ERP Implementation: Chief Information Officers' Perceptions of Critical Success Factors'. International Journal of Human-Computer Interaction. 16(1). 5–22.

Roberts, Darryl and Rollins, Thomas (1998). 'Work Culture, Organizational Performance, and Business Success: Measurement and Management'. Quorum Books.

Seddon, Peter B., Staples, Sandy, Patnayakuni, Ravi and Bowtell, Matthew (1999). 'Dimensions of Information Systems Success'. Communications of the Association for Information Systems. 2(20). November 1999.

Soh, C., S. S. Kien et al. (2000). 'Cultural fits and misfits: Is ERP a universal solution?'. Association for Computing Machinery. Communications of the ACM 43(4): 47-51.

Tarafdar, M. and R. K. Roy (2003). 'Analyzing the Adoption of Enterprise Resource Planning Systems in Indian Organizations: A Process Framework'. Journal of Global Information Technology Management 6(1): 31.

van Everdingen, Yvonne, van Hillegersberg and Jos Waarts, Eric (2000). 'ERP Adoption by European Midsize Companies'. Association of Computing Machinery online library.

Vogt, Christian (2002). 'Intractable ERP: A Comprehensive Analysis of Failed Enterprise-Resource Planning Projects'. Software Engineering Notes from ACM SIGSOFT. 27(2). March 2002. 62–8.

12. The Art of Public Sector Information Systems Management: The Role of the Task in Public Sector ERP Implementations

Carsten Svensson

INTRODUCTION

Information technology has become essential to all businesses operations. In many cases, success is determined by the ability to transform technological advances into enhanced enterprise performance.

Commercial organizations have in recent years been forced by market forces to continuously adapt their organizations through implementing and utilizing information technology (IT). Government organizations have also been under political pressure to implement enterprise resource planning (ERP) systems, but have not been able to take full advantage of the opportunities offered by IT, despite the similarity of objectives. This chapter suggests that a major contributor to the lack of success in government cross-functional IT implementations is an insufficient definition of the task prior to implementation, coupled with the fact that government organizations have been under pressure to implement solutions, not to succeed in implementations. As a consequence these organizations are unwilling to accept a high amount of risk, impairing their ability to implement IT systems successfully.

The government handles the most sensitive processes of the nation, often with inefficient and/or obsolete tools, resulting in exorbitant operating costs and a lack of responsiveness. In some cases the responsiveness of a government IT system can strongly influence the success or failure of a nation (Morales and Geary, 2003). This chapter will point to some of the shortcomings of the typical government first time ERP implementation.

Politicians and taxpayers often criticize the inefficiency of public sector IT implementations compared to those in the private sector. Public sector projects hire the same consultants, implement the same software and use the same methods, but the reported results of private industry have yet to be matched by the government. This chapter argues that a major factor contributing to the lack of success in government implementations is *precisely* that the public sector hires the same consultants, implements the same software and uses the same methods as the private sector.

It is a naïve and unsupported assumption that implementation tools are universal. A precise understanding of the task and its related constraints plays an important role in efficient government operations. All too often misguided managers rely on processes that have proven to be successful in industry without recognizing that their organizations have a different task. Consequently, incorrect methods have been applied correctly to a task that has not been identified.

The concept of a 'task' has been used frequently in management literature. Understanding and defining the task has proved to be useful, as failure is often linked to a poor definition of the task rather than a poor application of management tools. The lack of recognition of the individuality of the task has often led to a situation in which organizations are applying generic strategies without taking local context into account.

Point solutions have traditionally been preferred by government institutions because they can be implemented within one organization and with total control. This dramatically reduces the complexity of the implementation seen from a governance perspective however this is to the benefit of a *stovepipe*, not the enterprise. In government, an organization's IT systems have often been used with sophistication, often surpassing private industry to perform certain point tasks. The ability to integrate systems across the enterprise, however, falls behind private industry. Commercial industries have been under market pressure to adapt and take advantage of the opportunities offered through integration of information systems.

THE CONCEPT OF THE TASK

It is recognized that enterprises, government organizations as well as private sector companies, have a purpose and that they exist in an environment that cannot be fully controlled. The enterprise can control the internal systems through its behavior, and consequently the enterprises can adapt to the changing environment. However, Skinner (1978) acknowledged that organizations had difficulties aligning strategic goals and behaviors to adapt to a changing environment.

Skinner (1969), (1978) links the strategy to manufacturing through the concept of 'the manufacturing task', and this chapter argues that the concept of a manufacturing task is transferable to the public sector. By specifying the task before constructing the structural design of a system of business processes, it is possible to improve the fit between task and the applied strategy. The manufacturing task is defined by the following attributes (Skinner, 1969):

- Market,
- Products,
- Machines,
- Employees,
- Layout control,
- Customers, and
- Suppliers.

These variables may be supplemented with Leong et al. (1990), who incorporate the following strategic decision categories: facility capacity, technology, vertical integration, production planning, control, quality, organization, workforce, new product development and performance measurement systems. The decisions affect cost and quality.

Implementing ERP

The first step of implementing an ERP should be to identify the task the system supports, rather than identifying systems to replace. Task identification determines the outline of the solution, variance in attributes will vary from project to project, and especially from private sector to government. Most commonly the task is identified by coming to a shared understanding of the environment in which the organization operates and is based upon a precise definition of the organization's desired output.

Part of transforming a task into specific actions is to create a common operating picture. Without this picture there could be multiple interpretations of the same information. Most often the most effective way to create a common operating picture is through a graphical model. There exist several different tools on the market such as: ARIS, Popkin and IDEF. When the common operating picture and objectives are created it is possible to adjust the structure uniformly.

Ultimately, government organizations need a clear vision of the desired end state. Without this vision it will be difficult to progress through an implementation and in many cases one will end up doing the same work over and over again. However organizations often skip these conceptual steps, or are hesitant to change the existing environment.

Business processes

It is recognized that organizational redesign is a key to successful ERP implementations (Yusuf et al. 2004). For a government organization this is a significant hurdle because its paradigm is founded on stability. Government organizations are very difficult to change significantly. Most commonly, modern tools are applied but the way of doing business can often be traced back centuries. An ERP is not simply a tool that will support existing business processes, so consequently ERP implementations are not only a matter of applying a new tool to an old process, but rather is a matter of redefining the business and organization.

But redefining the business and organization is not attractive to those allergic to change. By default integrated enterprise systems promote centralization, which is a significant change implying giving up control. Control is the key to success in government management, hence managers are in most cases reluctant to sacrifice control for functionality.

In some organizations the information infrastructure is considered a tactical-level decision and consequently the dissemination of systems is often only local as the decision makers do not have an incentive to give up control, which promotes decentralization.

The Nature of ERP

The background for the lack of public sector ERP cases is not that public sector organizations have not invested in ERP, because they have. Our observations, however, indicate the investments have been decentralized, resulting in poorly integrated solutions. In the end, investments in IT have automated existing business processes, but have not realized the potential of integrated business process.

The single most common misconception about ERP is that ERP is a tool. In fact, ERP is a way of doing business as supported by an integrated information system. If ERP is approached as a tool, failure is imminent. At best outdated business processes will be automated and the organization will have an illusion of integration, which does not add value beyond perhaps decreasing maintenance costs.

To the disappointment of many users ERP implementations are not 'plug and play'. The process of designing and implementing ERP is a challenge and puts a strain on resources and is associated with undeniable risk.

In many cases claiming that one's business processes are unique is used as a defense against change, but change is what should happen when an ERP system is implemented. Changing the way an organization does business is the purpose of a software implementation. ERP offers users some tremendous advantages when seen from a global perspective, but there are trade-offs.

Overcoming the 'we cannot use the software if we have to change the way we do business' objection can be very difficult because some users will be forced to sacrifice local optimization for the common good.

Any ERP implementation should lead to the reinvention of the organization reflecting new opportunities and limits. Part of embracing the new organization is accepting that the old organization reflects another outdated reality, but government organizations have extreme difficulties overcoming this due to the stable nature of their business and lack of threats to their organization's existence.

In the literature, several attempts have been to identify the critical elements of a successful ERP implementation. Akkermans and van Helden (2002), for example, list the following critical elements:

- Top management support,
- Project team competence,
- Clear goals and objectives,
- Project management,
- Interdepartmental communication,
- Expectation management,
- Project champion,
- Vendor support, and
- Careful package selection.

Most organizations implementing ERP are aware of these critical success factors, but in many cases have difficulty moving from awareness to action. If the critical elements are not present, resources should first be focused on establishing the platform for an implementation rather than simply charging ahead.

THE CULTURE OF STABILITY

There is a difference in defining task and environment between the private and public sectors. Implementation consultants are often untrained in the differences in task and environment between the two sectors. To a new observer the antiquated structure of public sector information systems is often surprising. In many cases the public sector systems trail those in the private sector by at least five to ten years. This might not seem like a long time considering the time it takes to transform organizations with the size and complexity of government organization. In IT, however, five to ten years corresponds to several generations. For commercial companies it is not possible to be this far behind market leaders, as the company would have been forced out of the market.

Government organizations are by nature monopolies, providing the state with services focused on generating stability and functionality. There is very little encouragement of creativity, rationalization or change in other forms. The basic rule is, in many cases: 'If it ain't broke, don't fix it'. The relationship between risk and reward is not attractive compared to the exposure to criticism associated with failure. Consequently there is little incentive for change, and there is very little that can be done about this resistance, which makes government implementations particularly difficult. As long as day-to-day operational criteria are met middle management are typically very well-protected and autonomous. From an operational standpoint this gives governmental organizations a stable course and little interdependence. As a result, it is unlikely we will ever see a government Enron. The efficiency might not be world class, but a total meltdown is unlikely due to the autonomy. This ensures continuation but also poses some unique challenges regarding ERP implementations.

OBTAINING THE SKILLS FOR SUCCESSFUL IMPLEMENTATIONS

In government organizations individuals are highly mobile. A person often moves over several fields throughout a career. The most controlling dividing lines are hierarchical, which is a root cause of inefficiency. In many cases project members are appointed based on availability or seniority rather than on skills. To ensure efficiency government institutions must accept that the implementation of an information infrastructure is an expert task and assign personnel accordingly.

Modern information infrastructure is a highly specialized area and to be successful demands skills seldom acquired through working in a government institution. Most often the skill set is found in the private sector or at universities and at a senior level the mobility between the public sector and universities or the private sector is almost non-existent, so consultants are instead retained. In any organization there should be skilled personnel able match the skills of the 'hired help'. Only if the relationship between contractor and customer is equal will the potential of an implementation be realized.

Consultants are needed to support ERP implementations at the same time incompetent consultants are a recognized problem (Kumar et al., 2003)

A government organization must be critical when selecting advisors as there are large numbers of contractors offering their services, and often it is challenging for the customer to identify the competent bidders and at the same time comply with constraining acquisition legislation and regulations.

To some extent this expertise can be obtained from retaining consultancies, but the government must provide objectives and knowledge. At the end of the day consultants are there to help the government, but are not able to act as the government.

When large ERP implementations are planned in government the implementation organization often consists of government employees supported by consultants. Getting the correct government personnel can be difficult as the best are often already overworked, so in reality what can happen is the people an organization can easily spare (or would like to see leave) are sent, which can sabotage a project. Without the willingness to allocate the best resources available, the efforts are likely to be fruitless.

The method by which budgets are constructed makes it very difficult for government organizations to allocate dedicated resources. Resources are constrained and there are often limited resources and funds available to invest, a consequence of which is that it is difficult to dedicate competent personnel to a project. The organizational structure reflects a steady state, but this is a thing of the past, change is a constant in the private sector as well as public sector.

So does this mean government should invest in training personnel as part of an implementation? This is far from the optimal solution, because in most cases it would be too little too late. A comprehensive information infrastructure education cannot be completed within the timeframe that is typically available for education. Instead government should focus on hiring the right people. This might mean sacrificing some of the rigid organizational structures and maybe even incur extra cost, but this extra cost will be recuperated through a more efficient utilization of the consultants.

ERP implementations are a complex undertaking which challenge even the most competent. Finding the right people, getting training allocated, and ensuring continuity in the project team is in most cases extremely challenging due to the stovepipe nature of government organizations. Their performance measures are usually related to maintaining the status quo, and only rarely taking part in cross-organizational projects. As a consequence personnel assigned to these projects are not the top shelf, because the top shelf people will be assigned to the mission-critical task of meeting performance measures performing day-to-day operations.

Because change readiness is rarely a performance criteria for government leadership it is often difficult to approach a government leader who meets the performance measures for day-to-day operations, hence change can be perceived as an unnecessary risk in the career of a government leader.

CONCLUSION

The conclusion of this chapter is that public sector information infrastructure should not be managed in the same way as the commercial sector. It is most important to understand the task of the system and then implement in consideration of the environment, whether commercial or government. Government and private sector implementations are influenced by the same factors, but the environments are different so the allocation of efforts are significantly different, and it varies from organization to organization, but in general, more emphasis should be placed on organizational aspects and collaboration.

ERP systems are different from other IT systems from a process perspective. Their integrated nature is disruptive to existing stovepipes, which leads to uncertainty among leaders as they cannot fully control their domain. Integration cannot be accomplished post-implementation, it must be put into the design at a very early stage and rigorously enforced.

In government organizations, change is most often voluntary, which is a major barrier because progress is difficult when change cannot be enforced efficiently. In the public sector it is very difficult to force action as long as any relevant party is perceived to perform well by maintaining status quo, and eliminating personnel is close to impossible, with the exception of criminal acts. In the private sector changes are the order of the day, and change readiness is enforced to a degree where reluctance and elimination go hand in hand. This is not possible in government, so instead a much larger effort must be made the ensure stakeholder buy-in.

Before initiating an ERP implementation any public sector organization should evaluate the current state of its success factors and identify which resources should be allocated to prepare for a successful implementation prior to initiating the implementation. It must be recognized that implementing ERP is one of the most challenging efforts any organization can perform, and hence processes, organization and self-perception will be changed. In government ERP implementations consultancies play a key role. It is critical that the government select the right consultants and utilize them to their full potential. They cannot do the job of the government, but with sufficient support they can definitely support the implementation process. The government, however, should make an effort to become a competent customer.

If an implementation is to be successful the consultants must be empowered and the sponsoring organization must have the ability and willingness to sanction inappropriate behavior. ERP projects cannot be based on consensus or volunteering, as for some parts of the organization ERP will make life more difficult. Conformance to the best interests of the organization is needed if the implementation and the organization are to succeed as a whole, but this is unlikely to happen until the people of an ERP implementation are willing to sacrifice their own convenience for the greater good of the organization.

BIBLIOGRAPHY

Akkermans, H., Helden, K. van (2002): Vicious and virtuous cycles in ERP implementation: a case study of interrelations between critical success factors, European Journal of Information Systems, 2002, No. 11, 35-46

Kumar, Cinod, Maheshwari, Bharat and Kumar, Uma (2003): An investigation of critical management issues in ERP implementation: empirical evidence from Canadian organizations, technovation no. 23.

Leong, Keong, Ward, Peter and Snyder, David (1990): Research in the Process and Content of Manufacturing Strategy , International Journal of Management Science, vol. 18, no. 2, pp. 109-122.

Morales, Diane and Geary, Steve (2003): Speed Kills, supply chain lessons from the war in Iraq, Harvard Business Review.

Skinner, W. (1969): Manufacturing: missing link in corporate strategy, Harvard Business Review, 2. pp. 139–46.

Skinner, W. (1978): Manufacturing in the corporate strategy, Wiley-Intersciense Publications.

Yusuf, Yahaya, Gunasekaran, A. and Abrhorpe, Mark S., (2004): Enterprise information systems project implementation: a case study of ERP in Rolls-Royce, International journal of production economics vol. 87.

Wood, Thomaz and Caldas Miguel P. (2001): Reductionism and complex thinking during ERP implementations, Business Process Management Journal, vol. 7 no. 5.

Index